THOMAS MANN

In the same series:

BERT BRECHT *Willy Haas*
ALBERT CAMUS *Carol Petersen*
WILLIAM FAULKNER *Joachim Seyppel*
MAKSIM GORKI *Gerhard Habermann*
GÜNTER GRASS *Kurt Lothar Tank*
HERMANN HESSE *Franz Baumer*
JAMES JOYCE *Armin Arnold*
FRANZ KAFKA *Franz Baumer*
THOMAS MANN *Arnold Bauer*
EUGENE O'NEILL *Horst Frenz*
EZRA POUND *Jeannette Lander*
JEAN-PAUL SARTRE *Liselotte Richter*

Modern Literature Monographs

THOMAS MANN

Arnold Bauer

Translated by ALEXANDER
and ELIZABETH HENDERSON

Frederick Ungar Publishing Co.
New York

Translated from the German *Thomas Mann* by arrangement with the original publisher, Colloquium Verlag, Berlin

838
B

Contents

1

The Divided Bourgeois

Property and culture were synonymous during the age of the middle classes in the late nineteenth century. In the then already legendary world of Goethe, universal knowledge had been the ideal of perfect humanity. Universality was the mark of the fully mature personality, which Goethe had extolled as the highest happiness on earth.

Progressive specialization, in a world ruled by industrial technology's division of labor, set the signposts pointing toward a new human image, that of the mediator and manager, the coordinator and cooperating planner. In this world the creative personality became suspect. The present-day "social utopias" of both hemispheres deny human individuality and treat it as unreal, in the one case in practice and in the other in the theory of dialectical materialism. Old-style humanism is regarded as hopelessly antiquated. The new principles of collective order at best acknowledge some sort of "practical humanism."

The crisis of society reveals itself as a crisis of the individual, to the extent that he tries to comprehend himself as a unique being. This crisis, which encompasses also a crisis in the old concept of culture, began even before the profound shocks and upheavals of the twentieth century's wars and civil wars.

The middle classes of the twentieth century have lost their self-reliance and self-confidence; they are torn by inner conflicts. The most alert and sensitive minds among the bourgeoisie started to become aware quite early, from around the turn of the century, of the shadows that the coming catastrophes cast before them. Thus Thomas Mann's first novel, the work of a young man who saw himself as decadent, was written with forebodings of disasters to come. He was only twenty-four when he wrote *Buddenbrooks*, yet it counts as one of the lasting documents of *fin-de-siècle* literature. In it a young man presented a comprehensive diagnosis of decline, pointed to the possibility of survival and at the same time introduced, by its form, a concept of fictional writing that was to permeate his whole life's work, in which observation of himself and observation of the world mutually penetrate each other.

As a writer of fiction, and soon of analytical and polemical essays as well, Mann showed himself as keenly perceptive of change and crisis as were the cultural philosophers. He strove to master in prose narrative the sense of looming crisis, the social and existential problems of his time, and in so doing was always conscious of himself as subject to change and crisis. His heroic undertaking might be epitomized by a remark about the "work of anguished soul-searching," as he himself described his *Betrachtungen eines Unpolitischen* [Reflections of a Nonpolitical Man]: "No one remains entirely what he is as he comes to know himself."

This is the source of Mann's ironic detachment vis-à-vis himself and his contemporaries. The feeling of detachment makes him doubt himself and others. The constant readiness to be skeptical constitutes the greatness, but also the weakness, of an epochal mind. Yet Mann's *oeuvre*, though full of doubts, represents, probably for the last time, the moving effort—one that really exceeds human capacity—to draw an over-all picture of the European in an age which was no longer predominantly conditioned by European traditional and cultural values.

The language and techniques of composition employed by him in his daring undertaking display, from his earliest publication to his last, an unmistakable musical harmony, even though his instrumentation underwent continuous change. Between the traditional style of contemporary realism and the chronicle form of his first novel, and the experimental novels of a disrupted consciousness and of associative monologizing, Mann worked through a wide gamut of narrative forms and style. But the basic melodic theme, one of ironic statement and sad farewell, remained unaltered throughout. An arch spans the distance between the earliest short stories and the *Confessions of Felix Krull, Confidence Man.* Its pillars rest on the still unfathomed polarities of art and life, love and death. The strength of that arch, however, derives from a clear, cool, indeed altogether rational humanity. Mann's humanity is pliant but uncompromising, tireless in its questioning and searching, strong in doubt but strong also in its faith in the immanent powers of conscience and goodness.

2

Buddenbrooks

When Mann received me for an interview in the lobby of his Zurich hotel in June 1949, our talk was interrupted by a little girl, dressed in white, who presented him with a bouquet of flowers, together with best wishes for his birthday—"a perfectly ordinary seventy-fourth," as he explained. The child was a great-granddaugther of Richard Wagner.

The composer's name gave me a cue: "You are still greatly esteemed in Germany."

Thomas Mann replied: "Well, some people think I'm passé. Yet my *Buddenbrooks,* although it's almost fifty years old, is still alive and kicking."

And this is true. This family chronicle, which, after all, is rather sad and, in the words of its author, rests on "satirical characterization and pessimistic metaphysics," has retained its captivating freshness, even though, paradoxically, it carries a taint of decay—that sympathy with death that the young Thomas Mann, as a reader of Schopenhauer, felt as strongly as the affirmation of life, indeed an ecstatic intensification of the zest for life, which drew him to Nietzsche. To Nietzsche the poet and subtle master of language, that is, rather than to the philosopher of *Beyond Good and Evil.*

The success of *Buddenbrooks* is one of the most astonishing facts of modern literary history. Millions of copies have been sold, and it is one of those novels that have a place on the shelf of every middle-class German family. As long ago as 1923 the movies bought the story (the director was Gerhard Lamprecht). Quite recently Thomas Mann's best seller was made into a new film, which, with its less sophisticated treatment, insured the success of the "old family album" with a mass public that can only be reached by "pictures."

There is much to suggest that *Buddenbrooks* owes its enduring success to a misunderstanding, a misinterpretation against which Mann hardly ever protested. Far from it. The fact that his first novel was taken as evidence of patrician pride conveniently suited his later desire for "representativeness." His first reaction was a defensive one. When some of Lübeck's citizens felt deeply offended after *Buddenbrooks* appeared, Mann denied having written a *roman à clef*. He invoked the example of Turgenev and Goethe, who had not freely invented their stories but based them on reality.

"When I began to write *Buddenbrooks*, I was living in Rome. . . . My native town was not very real to me, in all truth; I was not really convinced of its existence. The city and its inhabitants were hardly more than a dream for me, a ludicrous and venerable dream dreamed long ago, dreamed by me and in the most particular manner my own." This is what the author himself confessed in 1906 in *Bilse und ich* [Bilse and I]. In 1925, at the invitation of the city fathers, proud of Lübeck's famous son, he delivered an address at the city's 700th anniversary celebrations. In his talk he was courteous enough to declare that as a writer he had always felt himself a son of Lübeck, and that it was not only in his first novel that he had stood up for Lübeck's "patrician civic spirit, for what was proper to Lübeck's status or generally Hanseatic." Mann's ambivalence toward the world of his origins, the childhood that had become "unreal," and its dreams, is shown in the two statements—the one (in 1906) disowning traditional ties and the later (in 1925) respectful, ironic bow. Both attitudes, however contradictory they may seem, were genuine.

This ambivalence, which can rightly be described as love-hate, contributed much to the book's astonishing success with readers. The public was entranced with the Biedermeier "family album," with the exuberant, even luxurious descriptions of the milieu, and overlooked the reflection of decadence and the inherent criticism of bourgeois society.

Until *Buddenbrooks,* Thomas Mann was known only to a few connoisseurs as a satirical short-story writer. Had he stuck to his first outline and, as originally planned, written a short novel of the suffering and death of little Hanno, in the concise style, say, of the Scandinavian impressionists, he would have probably done little more than arouse the attention of the literary public in the narrow sense.

Today, we would not wish to be without a single line of *Buddenbrooks*; we love the work in its full extent, with its enormous, yet orderly host of characters. In the gentle mockery, the brittle melancholy of the family chronicle, we are made aware of the old bourgeois heritage, of the flow of anecdotes and stories handed down from generation to generation. But what was supremely important to the young author of the book was the tragedy of the last member of the family, of the boy who playfully takes a ruler and draws a double line to mark the ending in the family record book.

Little Hanno, the boy estranged from brutal reality and intoxicated with music, is the real key figure of the novel. And he is *not* autobiographical in character, but points to a possible development avoided by one who was absorbed by life. In creating Hanno and allowing him to die, the writer, who was also a solid burgher, freed himself from the germ of morbidity within him.

While the family chronicle, spanning three generations, is a masterpiece of classical realism, a "merchant's ledger of German literature," as a critic described it decades ago, the heart of it really lies in the last part written in the style of a romantic novella.

The cool objectivity of the chronicle and of the humorous, occasionally satirical period piece stops short at this vital section; here the rhythmical prose turns into subjective poetry, into melody sounded as a leitmotiv. A poetic paraphrase of philosophy takes over; Schopenhauer's metaphysics provides a justification for discarding the social conventions as well as self-assertion in economic competition. Art appears as an opponent of the sort of life that existing society has to offer. Before the point of dissolution is reached, which is realistically exemplified in the liquidation of the old grain-trading firm, little Hanno, the frail, unfit and "marked" child, has to suffer the toughening-up tortures of the new German middle-class school system.

The critical chapter on education is symbolic of the imperialist, late-bourgeois Germany of the "silver age of Bismarck," which the historian Friedrich Meinecke contrasted unfavorably to the "golden age of Goethe." The school, the old *Gymnasium* which Hanno attends, has become a barracks. Thomas Mann devotes no less than seventy-six pages to his pamphlet, disguised as literature, against the then prevailing school system, as exemplified in the "institute." Its teachers almost without exception belong to the realm that a child's nightmares spring from. One might almost be tempted to accuse the author of spiteful distortion, were it not that contemporary school reformers denounced the late-bourgeois school system with equal sharpness.

Even the representative of the third generation, Senator Thomas Buddenbrook, the "man of knowledge" in the family, was, notwithstanding his zealous application to business, a man of fine nervous fiber, a spineless bourgeois, a bourgeois with a bad conscience. But the youngest and last in the line is wholly incapable of holding his own in the real world.

The romantic theme of flight into dream and death is sounded, first in musical, metaphysical terms, and then, with remarkable perception, in those of biological and psychological analysis.

In that same period, in which was published Sigmund Freud's first great book, *The Interpretation of Dreams,* a book noticed by only a few fellow experts, and twenty years before Freud conceived of the death instinct, Mann, at twenty-five, poetically anticipated, in little Hanno's musical ecstasy, the vision of inner destruction and self-annihilation.

There was something brutal and obtuse, and at the same time something ascetically religious, something like faith and self-sacrifice, in the fanatical cult of this nothing, of this scrap of melody, this short, childish, harmonic invention of a bar and a half . . . something vicious in the immoderation and insatiability with which it was enjoyed and exploited, and something of cynical despair, of a will to bliss and ruin, in the avidity with which the ultimate sweetness was sucked from it, to the point of exhaustion, of disgust and excess, until at last, at last in weariness, after all the extravagances, the ripple of a long, soft arpeggio was heard in a minor key, rose by a tone and resolved itself in the major, to die away in wistful hesitation.

A few lines after the verbal music that is the author's prelude to Hanno's trance at the piano and the final phase of a psychogenic process of dissolution, there follows the medically precise description of Hanno's exitus, once more abruptly invaded by metaphysics:

What happens with typhoid* is this: Into the distant feverish dreams, into the patient's burning forlornness, life is called in with an unmistakably encouraging voice. Hard and fresh, that voice will reach the spirit on the alien, torrid way on which he walks forward, and which leads to shade, coolness, and peace.

The author, a reader of Schopenhauer, a pupil of Flaubert and the Goncourt brothers, a man deeply stirred and haunted by the "holy literature of Russia," by the universal prose of Tolstoy and Dostoevsky, followed the call of the hard and fresh voice. But the beginning of his road to a life of work and fame, of the pain of being himself, of "the unfortunate abundance of inner conflicts" and of tribulation under the abuse of humanity's enemies, this beginning was, in a very real sense, completion.

Buddenbrooks is, in fact, a masterpiece complete —a masterpiece not only of Mann's but of modern fiction as a whole.

There is a classical quality about this novel. That is to say, it is artistic, objective documentation. Nothing

---

*Hanno's symptoms are characteristic of typhoid, though his sickness is less accurately labeled as typhus in English translations.—*Translators.*

purely self-centered can ever be classical. *Buddenbrooks* is perhaps the last great classical, artistically rounded, consistently and continuously narrated German novel. Essayistic reflection, psychology, associative monologue, "swimming in the ocean of language," as a young American follower of Hemingway said, hardly have anything in common any more with the classical form of the novel. This form was discarded by Marcel Proust, Robert Musil, Hans Jahnn, Franz Kafka, William Faulkner, Albert Camus, and Ernest Hemingway. Even Mann never adhered to the classical conception of the novel as fully in any of his later books as he did in his first major work. It looks as though the tremendous effort had exhausted his original intuition and had thrown him back upon himself. Thereafter, he wrote novelistic essays and essayistic novels, which displayed creative language, were carried to epic dimensions, and formed a soliloquy conducted with the most meticulous scrupulousness to the very end. Even a man of creative gifts, an artist in words, cannot in the long run escape the limitations imposed by the state of consciousness of the age which has made him.

With regard to the publication and fate of the great novel of Mann's youth, a few further points may be worth mentioning. The publisher, S. Fischer, and his editors had serious misgivings about the size of the manuscript, written in longhand, that they received. They did not think a two-volume novel would sell at all well. But the author resisted the suggestion of drastic cuts so vehemently and with such cogent arguments that the publisher eventually gave in.

While, in 1900, Mann was waiting with consuming impatience for the publisher's contract in the form he wanted, he was living in a barracks—fortunately only for a little while. "The shouting, waste of time, and iron trimness tortured me beyond description." The grind of the barracks yard, from which a medical certificate released him, may well have strengthened Mann's determination to yield no ground in the bargaining.

As the publishers had foreseen, the critics took exception to the length and scale of the two-volume work, which cost twelve marks. Even Arthur Eloesser, later Mann's first biographer, thought the first part of the family chronicle much too long. On the whole it was a *succès d'estime*, but in 1903, when the bulky one-volume edition of the novel was published, it led to triumph.

3

The Perpetual Autobiographer

Thomas Mann left no voluminous memoirs, but he did write an autobiography. It is the only authentic documentation of his life and it consists of the totality of his books, with the exception of *Buddenbrooks,* which constitutes the prehistory. The autobiographical thread is perceptible even in his speeches, contributions to periodicals, and biographical essays on others and, indeed, in his letters and replies to questionnaires. In these reminiscences of his own life, which are often, as it were, in code, though sometimes quite clear, an individual speaks to us without having recourse to dubious objectivity. Nevertheless, Mann's concern with himself is not monomania and seldom vanity before a mirror. Even when the author unabashedly identifies with one of his characters, this is anything but a case of secret wish fulfillment of his own ego. What happens, rather, is that the author writes a thoughtful commentary on these characters, with a twinkle in his eye, as it were, as though he meant to say: "This is exactly what would have happened to me, this and nothing else is what I would have done, too." And Mann always admitted his mistakes.

Yet his writing and striving are not, as they are with Ibsen or Tolstoy, a matter of sitting in judgment upon himself. What troubled him perennially was simply the Socratic question, that is, he had an eternal curiosity about himself. And thus he became the impassioned observer of his own life. The question Who am I always interested him more than the question of whence and whither. He shunned no effort in exploring the complex factors that conditioned his existence. He made himself a learned empiricist and formulated the existential question not so much in ontological as in

16

historical and sociological terms—or, as in the main work of his middle years, *Der Zauberberg (The Magic Mountain)*, in biological terms; or in mythological ones in the Joseph tetralogy; and, at the end of much self-reflection, even in medical and anthropological terms. In this sense his manifold autobiographical efforts add up, on an often more than popular-science level, to a survey of the knowledge of man in his time.

Seldom perhaps has anyone devoted so much disciplined industry, erudite study, and analytical technique to the creative investigation of himself. Because Mann, who always regarded his mission as that of a "representative" rather than that of an apostle, was predominantly interested in his own personal frame of reference, he incidentally furnished a far from negligible contribution to the social history of Germany in Kaiser Wilhelm's time, under the Weimar Republic, and in exile. No professional scholar should overlook this careful record of social studies that Thomas Mann conducted on himself.

It should detract nothing from the value of the authenticity of Mann's empirical findings that he mostly built them into the exquisite architecture of his great edifice of fiction. With an astonishing sense of proportion, he fitted the all but immeasurable sum of his findings into an artistically conceived plan of work and life. Such a degree of long-range planning and formal disposition sometimes borders almost on presumption. For Mann was no seer, no metaphysical poet, even though he liked to flirt with metaphysical categories (which caused some of his adversaries to deny his status as a creative writer). He was no ecstatic visionary; he was an erudite artist with a thorough appreciation of his powers, which all his life he carefully husbanded. This economy of his own powers was not the least of the sources of the sometimes seemingly irrational self-confidence of the rationalist Thomas Mann.

Four personal statements from four different phases of Mann's life turn spotlights, as it were, on his work. Alongside many other self-revelations, these four, widely spaced in time, are of existential significance. They are: 1907: *Im Spiegel* [In the Mirror]; 1930: *Lebensabriß* (*A Sketch of My Life*, Paris, Harrison, 1930); 1949: *Die Entstehung des Doktor Faustus: Roman eines Romane* (*The Story of a Novel: The Genesis of Doctor Faustus*, 1961); and 1950: *Meine Zeit* (*The Years of My Life*, *Harper's Magazine*, 1950).

Im Spiegel is the title of the detailed biographical reply of Thomas Mann (then thirty-two years old) to a magazine questionnaire. It is dictated by the playful high spirits of a young and successful novelist. Not with hidden irony as elsewhere, but with open derision, the author of *Buddenbrooks* scoffs at the moralizing respectability of his former teachers and his compatriots, who only ten years earlier had prophesied his "certain downfall." In grim triumph he writes:

I have a dark and disreputable past. . . . First, I was a flop in high school. It wasn't that I failed to pass my graduation exams—I would be bragging if I said that. The fact is I never even got as far as the top grade; even in the one below I was as old as the hills. Lazy, obdurate and full of dissolute scorn of the whole thing, odious to the teachers of the venerable institute . . . and at best enjoying a certain reputation with a few fellow students on account of some superiority hard to determine.

Mann was still quite young when he lost the benefit of paternal guidance. Senator Heinrich Mann died when his second son, Thomas (born on June 6, 1875), was fifteen. The older son, Heinrich, had already chosen a writer's career. Thomas had originally been meant to succeed his father as head of the grain-trading firm at Lübeck but, after the liquidation of the old family business, he followed his mother and her other children to Munich in 1893. At first he worked as an unpaid apprentice clerk in a fire-insurance company, but soon gave up this job and became a part-time student at Munich University. He attended lectures on history, economics, the history of literature, and aesthetics.

After Mann's first short stories appeared in 1894 and 1896 and were well received (the poet Richard Dehmel was one of the first to admire and support the new talent), the young writer decided to devote himself exclusively to his literary plans. He joined his brother Heinrich in Italy. While Heinrich Mann, spellbound by the Latin civilizations, chose a Mediterranean setting for his early novels and stories, Thomas, virtually untouched by southern influences, began in Rome to write his northern family chronicle.

With the same graceful impudence that a few years later became the hallmark of his Felix Krull (in the first fragment of the novel), the now socially acceptable "confidence man" proffers society his full contempt in his own person. Some of what he says in *Im Spiegel* is obvious bragging. With altogether improper indiscretion he boasts of his fortunate circumstances, describes in detail what an excellent marriage he has made and how splendidly he has furnished his

home. He talks of the autograph hunters who pester
him, including "lieutenants and young ladies," and
wonders how a "wayward fellow" could ever have
come so far:

. . . a charlatan, childish at heart, given to dissipation and
disreputable in every respect, who should have nothing to
expect from society but silent contempt, and actually ex-
pects nothing else from it. But it is a fact that society
makes room in its midst for men of such ilk to achieve a
respectable standing and an exceedingly comfortable life.

Mann concludes with an ironically moralizing
punch: "I'm not complaining. I get the best of it, but
it isn't right. It's bound to encourage vice and offend
virtue." If one did not know that this cynical confession
was penned by the young author of a novel full of
veiled social criticism as well as of a number of satirical
short stories, one might think they were the words of
a dandy. But Mann had taken the measure of the intellectual and social situation of his age. He knew that
nothing but solid affluence legitimized the artist's position as an outsider. Aesthetic virtuosity afforded a pre-
text for tongue-in-cheek moral mockery. As long as
the rules of the game of propertied society were not
seriously threatened, artistic satire was not only tol-
erated, but appreciated.

Mann's description of himself would have been
just right for *Simplizissimus,* on the editorial staff of
which he had worked for a time from 1897 on, and
which first published some of his early short stories,
such as *Tobias Mindernickel* (*Tobias Mindernickel*) and
Der Weg zum Friedhof (*The Path to the Cemetery,*
also *The Way to the Churchyard*). Later, Mann himself

said that his connection with the foremost satirical review of Germany had not been without its inner logic.

Impressionism was one of the last culminating achievements of late-bourgeois European civilization. One of its spokesmen, Richard Hamman, called the magazine, which was more than a comic paper, a "vehicle of impressionist culture." It was impressionism, penetrating beyond the visual arts to nearly all spheres of life, which at last gave a chance to the aesthetes and reformers, the moralists and protagonists of decadence from among the elite of bourgeois society itself. More than ten years after he fell silent, the moral impressionist Friedrich Nietzsche, the breaker of the old tables of values, at long last aroused the echo he had vainly longed for.

Young Thomas Mann's prose drew the consequences of the "transvaluation of all values." He was perhaps the last in the glittering row of "modern minds" at whose head stood Georg Brandes, professor of literature at Copenhagen and the first of Nietzsche's advocates (among their European ancestry may be mentioned the egotist Stendhal and the nineteenth-century critic and historian Hippolyte Taine).

"To realize one's nature perfectly—that is what each of us is here for." This somewhat Nietzschean pronouncement was made in *The Picture of Dorian Gray* by Oscar Wilde, who both conformed to Victorian hypocrisy and was its antipode. In France, a little later, André Gide, a distinguished young Protestant and ardent admirer of Nietzsche, wrote a novel whose theme is implicit in its title, *The Immoralist*.

All these modern minds looked for and found, irrespective of their different national origins, the style of a unitary European cultural awareness. Their extreme individualism was a declaration of war. Their often narcissistic self-reflection mirrored the late-bourgeois epoch. In the context of a dialectical moralist's and aesthete's retrospective social criticism, Georg Lukács wrote:

Thomas Mann is an extreme type of those writers whose greatness consists in being a mirror of the world. It is not that he is a dilettante in philosophy or a man lacking logical consistency of thought. Quite the contrary. In the bourgeois Germany of his time he has the culture of the thinker in the highest degree.

4

Interim Stocktaking

We do not know why Thomas Mann chose in 1930, of all years, to write the hitherto most extensive autobiographical commentary on his work. It bears the unpretentious title *Lebensabriß* (*A Sketch of My Life*) and was published in the July 1930 issue of *Die Neue Rundschau*. There is nothing to suggest that the article was commissioned. Since with Thomas Mann private and general motives were always intermixed, it may be assumed that the year of his twenty-fifth wedding anniversary, which followed the year he was awarded the Nobel Prize, was sufficient reason for him.

A Sketch of My Life, which marks one of the high points in his career as a writer, begins strictly chronologically and soberly, sounding like the personal history of someone presenting himself for an examination. It omits no date. His home, school, his spell as an unpaid apprentice clerk, his military service, his first attempts to establish himself as a writer, his friendships, hints of erotic longings, his reading and travels—all this is recorded faithfully and sometime dryly. It is only with hesitation that the autobiographer applies stylistic polish, that he strikes the note of self-irony and parody. But the very abundance of facts in this text, along with a relative parsimony of formal elaboration, affords a particularly good approach to the labyrinth of a life's work, variously encoded, which, by that time, had grown to numerous volumes in S. Fischer's light gray linen bindings.

The stocktaking is comprehensive. It tests the products of lasting value, provides information on formal means, reveals the psychological and intellectual reaction of the author to his early and—on that scale—unexpected success, and it examines how art and life interweave in individual instances. The backward

look is clear and cool, untroubled by any kind of senti-
mentality:

I had proved myself; my obtuse resistance to the conventional claims of the world was vindicated, society took me
up—to the extent that I allowed myself to be taken up;
society was never very successful in these efforts.

On one level *A Sketch of My Life* is a chronicle
of the family founded by himself. Mann describes all
the circumstances surrounding the "social occasion" of
his marriage in 1905 to Katja Pringsheim, the daughter
of a well-to-do university professor, who lived in great
style and displayed a special bent for music. Mann does
not mention that it was a Jewish family, a fact that
he by no means concealed in his short story *Wälsungenblut* [The Blood of the Walsungs]. But that *nouvelle
à clef* was withdrawn at his father-in-law's wish even
before it appeared. After the First World War a French
translation of it was published by Grasset in Paris.

After his marriage Mann's prosperous home became the representative background of his literary
work. The refined fruit of such highly satisfactory
domestic circumstances was a second *roman à clef,
Königliche Hoheit (Royal Highness)*, which Mann
calls an "attempt at a comedy in the form of a novel."
Its theme was a "pact with fortune," with, as a topical
bonus, a compassionate analysis of the dynastic form of
life, which—in 1909, be it noted—was exposed as "an
institution ripe for its downfall." At this point he recalled *Tonio Kröger* (1903) and *Tristan* (1903), two
novellas which, like *Fiorenza* (1905), a Renaissance
drama of ideas and discussion, were written between
his first two full-length novels. He explained how, in
his fiction, he developed the leitmotiv of *Buddenbrooks*

in musical rather than in physiognomic and naturalistic terms. Only after *Buddenbrooks*, he commented, did he fully realize the influence of music in molding his form and style.

Of *Tonio Kröger* he spoke with some feeling. This story, he confessed, was closest to his heart, and the young still seemed to like to read it. (As late as 1949 he again spoke in very similar terms about it.) *Tonio Kröger* became important to Mann for other reasons besides the "musical transparency of emotions and ideas" for which he so highly prized it. This story opened a "romantic" phase in Mann's thinking and even more so, in his emotions, a romanticism vaguely inspired by his reading of Schopenhauer and by the music of Richard Wagner. But even more lasting, as it turned out, was the influence of Nietzsche's dithyrambic philosophy, which Mann compares with a "magic complex."

Just as Nietzsche, as the antipode of his century, in his heart's core owed much to Romanticism and ultimately reverted to it in the process of his gradual self-disintegration, so, under his conflicting stimulus, did Mann find himself again and again susceptible to the seductive charms of a romantic attitude to life, without ever quite yielding to them. His occasional inner concessions to the romantic glory of life and death are counterbalanced by the brave irony he adopted in regard to himself.

In *Tonio Kröger*, the contrast between art and middle-class convention is entirely conceived in the romantic vein. The protagonist hankers with "melancholy envy" for the vitality of the "blond beast," but they are tamed beasts, those fair-haired and blue-eyed creatures so brightly alive, the happy, lovable, and ordinary men for whom he harbors a secret love, the love of a writer still, at heart, regretting his lost ties with convention. Hans Hansen, Tonio Kröger's worthy counterpart, is readily recognizable as one of those well-brought-up and hearty young men "of good family." These blond and insipid worthies of a bygone generation provide Mann both with a target for romantically erotic irony and with an occasion for passing conservative approval on this German prototype.

Tonio Kröger, whose contradictions are announced in his very name, with its southern and northern origins, is one of those men of "typical ambivalence." With his longing for what is thoroughly alive (be it only a life of good manners) he can be taken as an example of the burgher with a bad conscience, just like Thomas Buddenbrook.

In *Tristan,* the author's critical observation of his own ego turns to self-mockery. While contemporary critics described *Tonio Kröger* as a mixture of Theodor Storm and Nietzsche, the only slightly later psychological study of the tragicomically self-divided man of letters and the unsatisfied young woman with the "beautiful soul" can be regarded as a fusion of Schopenhauer and Wagner in the form of a short-story theme. Herr Spinell, who conveys the impression that writing comes harder to a writer than to anyone else, is a piece of banter, carried to a grotesque level, at the expense of a type of literati not uncommon in Germany at the time.

Like Tonio Kröger, Spinell wears a two-faced mask, but Spinell's self-division is exaggerated to the point of caricature. On one side he is an aesthete and moralist; on the barely concealed other side he turns out to be a moral outsider who prostitutes his soul. In

confessions which are as confidential as they are eloquent, he bares his soul to the fair-haired nonentity he
adores, that tender figure of cobwebby vitality whose
husband, the prosperous businessman Klöterjahn of
Bremen, claims his rights on her mercilessly and
brutishly.

"Conscience, dear lady," Spinell said, ". . . It's a bad
business about conscience. . . . I and the likes of me have
our troubles with it all our life, and we have our work
cut out to propitiate it with small, cunning satisfactions.
. . . We hate the useful, we know that it is vulgar and un-
lovely, and we defend this truth as we defend only truths
which are absoutely essential to us. And yet we are so
eaten up by bad conscience that there's hardly a sound
spot left on us."

More patently than any other of his early works,
Tristan displays the power of music as a formative element in the style of Mann's writing, which in this
respect, too, leans toward the spirit of Romanticism.
According to the author himself, the application of
musical laws of style explains the almost pedantic
thoroughness and above all the slowness of his method
of work:

It is not a question of timidity nor of laziness, but one of
having an extraordinarily alert sense of responsibility in the
choice of every word, the turn of every phrase—a sense
of responsibility which requires one to be completely
fresh and makes one feel after two hours of work that one
would rather not tackle another sentence of any sort of
importance. But which sentence is "important" and which
one not? How can one know in advance whether a sentence,
or part of a sentence, may not be destined to recur, to
serve as a theme, parenthesis, symbol, quotation, or reference? And a sentence that is to be heard twice must be

phrased accordingly. I'm not talking of beauty, but it must possess a certain elevation and symbolic mood which makes it worth being sounded again in some future context.

Mann does not think his novel *Royal Highness*, "the first artistic fruit of my young married life," worth more than passing reference in *A Sketch of My Life*. He dissociates himself from it up to a point, by agreeing with those critics who found it too lightweight. The "sensible fairy tale" of the marriage of a German prince from a reigning dynasty to an American millionaire's daughter (a subject still somewhat utopian in 1909) clearly was an intermezzo. But, gay intermezzo as it was, it contained the germ of a social problem, as Mann points out in retrospect, after twenty-five years of married life:

There we had a young married man spinning a tale about the possible synthesis of solitude and companionship, form and life, about the reconciliation of an aristocratic, melancholy awareness with new claims such as might even have been epitomized by the word "democracy." His humorous fancies drew their mood from autobiographical sources and left aside any direct prophecy or special pleading.

Thomas Mann's brother Heinrich recognized it for what it was: "This is a profession of faith in democracy."

In 1910, a year after the appearance of *Royal Highness*, Mann's sister Carla took her own life. This dreadful occurrence is recalled in full detail, with compassion but also with indignation in *A Sketch of My Life*. It prompted him to make comments that tell us much about his personal view of the relationship of art and life—he asserted that the ironic view is superior to the reality of life and of the "terrible finality" of death, and came to the following seemingly contradictory or at least ambiguous conclusion:

In truth, I had no right to complain. For I myself had already become "real" to a large extent, by work and position, by home, marriage, and child, or whatever the affairs of life, serious or humanly pleasant, may be called; and if in my case becoming real meant blessings and gaiety, it was made of the same stuff as my sister's deed and implied the same disloyalty. Reality is always *deadly* serious, and it is morality itself, at one with life, which prevents us from remaining loyal to our youth that was untainted by reality.

Do not such sentences conceal an option in favor of art, of the "gay" illusion? An inner rejection of "life's earnestness," which ultimately includes that consensus of a society's values that goes by the name of "morality"?

It was no accident (but in this perspective it appears almost necessary) that during the year of Carla's death, which profoundly upset his elderly mother in particular, Mann should have begun his gayest work, one which he continued only in the last years of his life and which—perhaps equally not by accident—remained uncompleted, namely, *Bekenntnisse des Hochstaplers Felix Krull* (*Confessions of Felix Krull, Confidence Man*). Now, in 1930, having in the meantime become an adherent of Freud's theories, Mann interprets what he had published of *Felix Krull* as a "new facet of the theme of art and the artist," as "psychology of the unreal, illusionary form of existence."

Mann goes even further, to the point of radical self-disclosure, not to say exposure.

Stylistically what fascinated me was the hitherto untried autobiographical immediacy which my coarse-grained model suggested, and there was a fantastic attraction in the parodistical idea of transporting into criminal terms an element of cherished tradition, the Goethean self-descriptive and autobiographical, the aristocratic, confessional element.

There follows a sentence which lays bare Mann's sharpened awareness of his position—it might be defined as self-knowledge and the determination of his own standpoint—and tears away the veil of "bourgeois" pretenses:

It [*Felix Krull*] may in a certain sense be the most personal thing I ever wrote, for it treats of my attitude to tradition, which is at the same time affectionate and subversive, and which decides my vocation as a writer. The inner laws that later governed the evolution of my educational novel (*Bildungsroman*) *The Magic Mountain* were surely of kindred nature.

Felix Krull remained a fragment. Mann published parts in 1932, in a paper-covered edition brought out by the Deutsche Verlagsanstalt, Stuttgart (not, strangely enough, with his regular publisher S. Fischer), and in 1936. The final, still incomplete, version appeared in 1954, a year before Mann's death, with the subtitle *Memoirs Part I*, the last piece of his narrative writing to be published. For more than forty years this "most delicate balancing act," as he called it, occupied the author, at least to the extent of thinking about it, before he took it up again after his return to Europe from the United States.

In *A Sketch of My Life* Mann does not tell us why he interrupted for so long his work on these "confes-

sions." The theme of the confidence trickster must have
worried him a lot, for, "to get a rest from it," he went
on a trip to Italy with his wife in the spring of 1911.

The "secret lookout for new things" was to yield a
"productive idea." Its was realized in *Tod in Venedig*
(*Death in Venice*), published in 1912. While the *Krull*
fragment, until the 1954 volume, had always been
mentioned only incidentally and treated casually by
contemporary critics as well as by historians of literature (Marxist literary historians, as represented by
Georg Lukács and Hans Mayer, do not even acknowledge its existence), none of the Mann's shorter
fictional works has been so often commented upon,
analyzed and polemically discussed as the story of the
famous writer Aschenbach, surely Mann's most com-
plaisant self-portrait.

Certainly there is more self-complacency in the
claim to homage from a world deeply stirred and
mourning the death of its representative writer, whom
Mann endowed with certain traits of the composer
Gustav Mahler, than in the ingenuous narcissism of the
confidence man.

The way in which in this Venetian elegy Mann
brought his flirtation with death to its tragic end by,
so to speak, metaphysical main force, deeply impressed
the middle-class readers of the "golden" age before the
First World War. The public studiously overlooked the
strong inner relationship between the "frivolous" figure
of Felix Krull and the "venerable" one of Gustav
Aschenbach brought to destruction by his forbidden
desires.

Henry Hatfield, Thomas Mann's American biographer, has pointed out the inner connection between
Aschenbach and Krull. He regarded it as "a measure

of Mann's complexity" that he started work on *Death in Venice* immediately after interrupting *Felix Krull*, and added: "The most heroic portrait of the artist follows directly after the most scurrilous." In *A Sketch of My Life*, Mann recorded that during his work on *Death in Venice* he occasionally experienced "a feeling of a certain absolute transformation, of a certain sovereign exaltation."

Hatfield, who believed that the story comes close to the cool monumentality and the chiseled style of the poet Stefan George, calls *Death in Venice* the "least bourgeois" of Thomas Mann's works.

After nearly twenty years, Mann still registered with pride the deep impression which this story made:

In spite of its rather risqué subject, this book brought about a certain moral rehabilitation of the author of *Royal Highness* in the eyes of the German public, which really has no use for light reading and respects only what is serious and weighty.

But the form and content of *Death in Venice* also called forth objections and gave offense to petit-bourgeois moralizers.

5

The Nonpolitical Man

During the First World War Mann went through a phase of conservative thinking and patriotic feeling. Though conscripted into the reserves, he was actually spared army service. His only "military" exploits were his lectures at a few bases behind the front line. Mann was never to deny his conservative attitude at the time and alway admitted it to have been a necessary stage of crisis in his development. It was only in 1918, shortly before the end of the war, that Mann published his volume of essays on the philosophy of civilization under the title, as deliberate as it was unpretentious, of *Betrachtungen eines Unpolitischen*. The book is an essential document on the crisis of the traditionally nationalist German middle class, which wanted to be both liberal and humane; its whole insoluble inner conflict is here revealed as it was reflected in the conscience of an upright, intelligent man. This is why the *Betrachtungen* are more than an individual confession. They are, in advance of *The Magic Mountain*, a comprehensive statement of the ideas that dominated the waning bourgeois age.

Mann had worked on these essays for two years. Under the overpowering psychological pressure of the war, Mann lived through what was undoubtedly his own most profound personal crisis, as well as the crisis of an age. Never did Mann's complicated personality appear so "representative" of his time as in those years. In retrospect he spoke of this phase as one of thrashing about in a thicket without knowing his way, and of a torment with which he was alone. The only confidant of his political-antipolitical ruminations was, he says, Ernst Bertram, a professor of German literature, a member of the group around Stefan George, and the eloquent antagonist of Auguste Maurice Barrès in the debate about the "Génie du Rhin." These soliloquies, born of distress of spirit, said Mann, had been a rearguard action, and the Protestantism and conservatism with which his listener Bertram was all too familiar, were for himself more "the artistic conquest and exploration of the melancholy and reactionary sphere" than an expression of his essential nature.

The *Betrachtungen* has usually been misunderstood. The "reactionaries" have mistakenly praised and quoted it, the "progressives" have shaken their heads disapprovingly and have had nothing to do with it. In a cosmopolitan context of ideas cleansed of nationalistic dross, the irrational and national resentments here displayed were bound to seem alien, and indeed hostile. But the censorious critics often overlooked the fact that these resentments and irrational premises were questionable enough in the author's eyes, for otherwise he would never have undertaken this "thorough overhaul of [his] fundamental position."

At no point in this "strenuous soul-searching," moreover, did Mann debase himself to blind worship of Germany's bourgeois and imperialist claim to power. There is no need, therefore, for any subsequent "tactful" silence about his position or for justifications to remove any "embarrassment" that these *Betrachtungen* might have caused their author. Wherever this deeply pondered book is opened, whatever is quoted from it, there is not a word that can be subtracted from the wonderful harmonious whole of a life's work, nothing that does not testify throughout to Mann's sense of responsibility and to his intelligence. Does the following confession, as national as it is personal, really have anything in common with the customary blind faith and blind rage of German nationalism?

I shared the sense of destiny of the cultural elite of Germany, whose faith contained so much truth and error, right and wrong, at a time when Germany was facing such terrible lessons, even though they were, all in all, salutary and conducive to maturity and growth.

Frankly and self-critically Mann acknowledged the emotional sources of his attitude during the First World War:

The sharp sense of a turning point between two eras, one of which would inevitably deeply affect my personal life as well, had been with me from the outset—it was indeed at the root of that intoxication with destiny which made me take so emphatically German a stand in regard to the war.

"Intoxication with destiny." The remark was prophetic as well as profound. Only a keenly alert mind could escape being caught up in it, only merciless self-examination could prepare the conversion that came with self-knowledge. It was the turning of a "nonpolitical man" toward politics, toward the active politics of the thinking mind, which, in the final decision for or against the conscience of mankind, once and for all set Mann apart from those charlatans of intellectual half-measures, who did not have the courage to think things through consistently to the end, who assailed the mind as the antagonist of the soul, those politically innocent lambs who in the sequel fell prey to the rapacious power-seeking wolves.

For everyone rooted in bourgeois civilization the intellectual point of departure was the same as that of Mann (the Lübeck patrician's son), who frankly admitted that he was more indebted to moral and metaphysical traditions than to political and social ones.

But few of the German burghers realized as clearly
as did the author of *Buddenbrooks* that their decision
to be nonpolitical was itself a political one. Faced over
and over again with the alternative of being the upper
or the nether millstone, the German middle class opted
for the role of—onlooker. And those who laid claim
to a patent of nobility as "pure" intellectuals, isolated
themselves completely and, by the peculiar and es-
oteric form of their intellectual fellowship, prepared
the ground for an aristocratic leadership cult which
later found a plebeian counterpart on an entirely different plane. Mann had far too acute a conscience and
far too much irony toward himself to yield to the temp-
tations emanating from the emotional cult of those
circles to which the confidant of his nonpolitical reflections, Ernst Bertram, belonged. The stern exaltation
of a man like Stefan George was bound to be suspect
to the German skeptic Mann. But strange currents of
feeling and lines of thought connect the two worlds.
The circuit of man-to-man masculine eroticism, which
held the most distinguished minds in its spell, was as
propitious as it was fatal to German culture and Germany's destiny. Mann's attitude to it was one of detached criticism with an undercurrent of sympathy.
And it was this sympathy, in the last resort, which
interested some of the members of the George circle in
his work and which, in turn, enabled Mann to explore
the mysterious connections and tensions between mind
and life, which kept troubling the spirit in the classical
German renewal of the Platonic Eros. This is how
Mann almost inevitably came for a while close to those
intellectual circles which—strangely enough under the
sign of the sun-wheel—went in for a mystically un-
political and Platonic personality cult.

6

The
Magician

Mann was just about in the middle of his sixty-year writing span (1894-1955) when he completed his novel *The Magic Mountain,* the most densely charged with problems among so many books both rich in problems and problematical. Twelve years went into the making of this hermetic magnum opus.

He was again led to the subject "by chance," and he did not originally plan the work on a large scale. In 1912, Mann went to Davos to visit his wife, who had had a spot on her lung and was convalescing for a few months in the Swiss mountains.

Retrospectively, Mann described the genesis of *The Magic Mountain:*

In May and June 1912 I spent three weeks as a guest in the sanitarium with her [his wife] at Davos and collected—but the word is very inadequate for the passive way in which I soaked up experiences—those strange impressions of the milieu, out of which there developed the Hörselberg* idea as a compact novella. It was intended to be another quick insertion in my work on the confessions of a confidence man, which definitely still attracted me—a satyr play to the tragedy of degradation in the novella [*Death in Venice*] from which I had come.

It is interesting to note the renewed mention of *Felix Krull,* this favorite project of Mann's throughout most of his life, as well as his reference to the "tragedy of degradation."

The Magic Mountain marked Mann's inner break with the main body of the contemporary German middle class. He had gained detachment and had per-

*The Hörselberg, a mountain in Thuringia, is supposed to be the legendary Venusberg, the home in which Tannhäuser and Venus lived in pagan love for seven years.—*Translators.*

haps already said his farewell. All the greater was his surprise at *The Magic Mountain*'s success and at the positive response of the German public. He was astonished when his "problematical private amusement," the "dreamy intricacies of this 1200-page mosaic of ideas" met with so much appreciation. And, equally, he was amazed that so many people should be prepared to pay sixteen or twenty marks, which was a lot of money at the time, for such a "bizarre entertainment." Mann was optimistic enough to interpret this as a sign of his being in accord with the general trend of his age.

In *A Sketch of My Life* he wrote of "experiences that the author had in common with the nation" and observed:

The problems of *The Magic Mountain* were by nature not such as would interest the masses, but they were a burning issue to the educated classes, and the general misery had imparted to the receptiveness of the broad public precisely that alchemistic "intensification" which was the essence of little Hans Castorp's adventure.

Had Mann in 1930 been able to use methods of sounding opinion and investigating the social structure of the reading public, doubtless he could have saved himself many of the disappointments and self-deceptions that lay ahead of him.

The Germany with which he felt at one and in which indeed he thought he recognized himself, was that of the official, democratic, neobourgeois Weimar Republic. Germany at the time was a middle-of-the-road country, one of compromise, of bourgeois humanism supported by a liberal minority which, with regard to its attitude to life and the ideologies that determined its thinking, had nothing at all in common either with the bulk of the lower middle classes or with the thin upper crust that actually exercised power, and most certainly not with the proletarian masses. It was among this liberal minority of intellectuals (that is, neither those who voted the World War I field marshal Paul von Hindenburg into the presidency in 1925 nor the organized Socialist and Communist workers) that Mann could count upon the "sympathy of suffering."

The Magic Mountain was a work difficult to translate, but it made an impact on the European market once it had appeared in several languages— rather late, incidentally, in France, where this Germanic and romantic work with its metaphysics of death was hailed by André Gide in an emotional, and moving, letter to the author.

The case of the "mediocre" Hans Castorp, the Hamburg patrician's son whom fate landed in the high mountains, is an example of true intellectual development, in the course of which a young burgher, drilled in respectability and intellectually wholly untrained, acquires in a very delicate sense a subtle mind capable of detached reflection. Mann establishes a precedent: the motivation for this development is not the traditional world of middle-class education with its erudite mentors, but the illness into which the young man escapes from the lowlands of bourgeois occupations. Since Hans Castorp has enough money, he also has time—until ultimately "time" possesses him and he learns its relativity by realizing that it is not time that passes, but man who passes into time, which enfolds him mysteriously, incomprehensibly, impenetrably.

This mystical relativity of time, which has its scientific counterpart in Einstein's theories, is not an ingredient of traditional middle-class culture. It has to be personally experienced. The well-brought-up young man of Hanseatic stock loses all respect for the emotional and cultural values which are his heritage, because he now lives face to face with death. And death on the mountain does not make a formal and ceremonial appearence—it is no dignitary wearing the stately ruff of bourgeois tradition—but a commonplace and ordinary occurrence. The stigma of illness brings about a peculiar and heightened sensitivity unobtainable by the common educational means of an old, ossified culture. The illness, which casts its spell upon the young and barely resisting young burgher, provides insights into the dark depths of the human condition, beyond all the ties of profession, class and caste, money and status, but also beyond any identifiable period as determined by traditional science. Illness and death are quantities beyond human comprehension, which shatter the moral security of the decent average German burgher. Precisely this, too, is the author's skillfully concealed intention. Mann wishes to teach his "mediocre" hero *not* to take things for granted, especially not in the delusive shape suggested by "education" and "tradition"—only another name for laziness of the heart and mind.

Having thus deliberately and consciously created a set of artificial conditions entirely outside the normal, Mann uses them as the background against which powerful historical ideas—whether they are epitomized as democracy versus dictatorship or humanism versus nihilism is ultimately irrelevant to the author's ironic dialectic—fight for the soul of a German who is characterized as "average." Hans Castorp is exposed to a daring pedagogical experiment. What is at stake is the attempt to see if the spiritualization of man is at all

possible. The experiment, translated into the language
of politics, is an eminently democratic and humane
one.

The experiment, however, fails in the case of one
of Mann's other examples, Castorp's cousin Joachim
Ziemssen, the young officer. For him, the illness that
isolates does not become the catalyst of thought; he is
afraid of learning to understand his own problems. This
no doubt is the normal reaction. Joachim is the stolid
soldier, the eternal symbol of Prussianism with its rigid
dogma of duty. Unmistakably, he speaks the language
of the ideal officer of two world wars: "I'm telling you,
it doesn't matter what sort of opinions a chap holds,
so long as he's a decent fellow. The best thing is to have
no opinions at all, just to do one's duty." And Mann,
ironically, sets him up as a symbol. He mercilessly
sends him to his destruction by expelling him from the
magic mountain "uncured" (in an ironic double meaning) sending him to the "lowlands" to serve his country
and to die in so doing. His is a German destiny: the
unprotested destruction of "noble" mediocrity at the
command of an imperious voice.

Hans Castorp remains on the magic mountain.
Distinguished intellectuals, dignified representatives of
reasoned judgment, are marshaled, no less than the
mysterious forces of the irrational, to prepare him for
the greatest human experience which the cognitive
mind can at moments partake of—the experience of
humanity ruling itself and the world by its own free
mind and goodness, the aim both of those who yearn
for the Christian kingdom of God on earth and of those
who find this kingdom in the pages of the Communist
Manifesto. After a long novitiate in the school of two
unusual mentors—the amiable Settembrini, "civiliza-

tion's man of letters" from erudite Bologna, and the rigorous apostle of Jesuitical, absolute principles, the fanatical Herr Naphta from Galicia—Hans Castorp reaches the no man's land between death and life, where his soul enters upon its "reign."

In a brilliant chapter, mankind's old, eternal dream of a finer humanity is projected in the fading consciousness of Hans Castorp, as he is on the point of freezing to death, and here we find a sentence that the author caused to be printed in italics: *"For the sake of goodness and love, man shall not allow death dominion over his thoughts."* That is Mann's answer to German, and to European, nihilism.

With it, he finally surmounted Romanticism, the emotional expression of death's sovereignty. In the *Betrachtungen* and, earlier, in *Buddenbrooks* and even more so in *Death in Venice,* he was still entirely under the seductive spell of the romantic, mystic lay of love and death. In *The Magic Mountain* the sympathy with death, kept under formal control, degenerates into dissipation and debauchery, and thereby stands condemned. All the characters of *The Magic Mountain* are illuminated by the sunset glow of the decline of the old Europe. This applies in particular to the Venus of this mountain, the mysterious Russian lady Madame Clavdia, who is the imago of Hans Castorp's erotic dreams. She is all self-oblivious passion, yielding and elusive, a sphinx in the mask of a *grande dame,* suffering and enjoying her suffering.

Madame Clavdia's companion, the vital Mijnheer Peeperkorn, is one of the last burghers whose zest for life is still unimpaired. His spontaneous personality once more embodies the early spirit of enterprise of a past age. A man of strong feeling, he cannot bear the

shadowy spook of illness, the morbid rivalry with the
"patients," and he knows how to die majestically, as
befits a great Pan. It is said that Mann gave this regal
stammerer features modeled on those of Gerhart
Hauptmann's. These features are those of a naïve,
creative man, in whom the ideas and, even more
strongly, the sense of life of an epoch are reflected.
For Mann, on the other hand, this condition of reflect-
ing is a double one; it is like an actor playing a part
without suspecting that he is representing his own
destiny.

But the "simple" young man Hans Castorp contains
secretly not only a piece of Mann's own self, but a sub-
stantial slice of Germany's fateful tragedy—a tragedy
turned into tragicomedy by Mann's irony, one that
stops, in the novel as in historical reality, with a question mark. Mann leaves Hans Castorp at a moment
when it is still an open question whether Hans Castorp
will accept the teaching of Settembrini, the amiable
individualist and "organ grinder" of capitalist civilization, humanism, and progress, or of Naphta, the mystic
collectivist and fanatical inquisitor of a new absolut-
ism. (After the lessons of two world catastrophes the
"cheerless guest on this earth"—Naphta—can well be
described as a militant spokesman of totalitarianism.)
The two personifications of a divided *Zeitgeist,* ration-
alism and mysticism, have struggled for possession of
Hans Castorp, and Mann extricates himself from the
macabre affair of the magic mountain by means of a
dialectical answer to the eternal metaphysical question
What is the meaning of it all? His answer is that man
is the master of contradictions.

In the timeless atmosphere of the sanitarium, the entire stock of an era's ruling ideas and its cultural heri-

tage is once more skillfully paraded, and we get cultural philosophy and German metaphysics in the form of an intellectual novel. Not only are the physical processes of disease illuminated by radioscopy, but the foci of psychoses among nations and of cultural decline are also diagnosed. But Mann, who was all but unique in his comprehension of cultural life in this historical phase of social crisis, recommended no therapy. He distrusted the charlatans peddling "infallible" panaceas, and he did not offer his readers the gratification of any "philosophical" patent medicines. Detachment from his own self is the origin of the question with which his work, at the beginning of the great world conflagration, breaks off rather than comes to its conclusion, a question accompanied by the dying notes of a melancholy, romantic air: "And will love arise someday even from this world festival of death, from the heat of this bad fever, that sets the rainy evening sky ablaze all around us?"

7

*The
Public
Man*

Many efforts have been made, even in the most recent past, to take politics out of *The Magic Mountain,* the cornerstone of Mann's fiction, and to establish its irony as a classical example of Romantic irony. But the "ironic German" did not primarily have the ambitious intention of creating "progressive universal poetry" after the model of Friedrich Schlegel. Mann meant neither to mix nor to fuse "poetry and prose, invention and criticism."

By his own testimony, the great essays in which he openly, and indeed with polemical cut and thrust, upheld bourgeois humanism and the new republic's internationally minded attitude, were "direct critical offshoots of the novel."

He talked of his "polemical bent" as of an inalienable ingredient of his nature. I am reminded of a sentence from *Betrachtungen eines Unpolitischen*: "I have never, in terms of values, regarded myself as an 'aesthete,' but always as a moralist."

Among these attempts to reconcile spiritual values and national feeling, Mann's address *Von deutscher Republik (The German Republic)*, delivered in 1922, occupies a special position. Though fundamentally averse to emotionalism, he for once employed fiery and forceful words in a more than usually open profession of faith in a higher humanity. Delivered on the occasion of Gerhart Hauptmann's sixtieth birthday to an audience of students, this address amounts to a great argument with current attitudes, then still wavering between extremes. Its significance far transcends the topicality of the national themes discussed and reaches well into the future.

Mann's speech (which is really a classic essay)

was not an attempt at an apologia intended to rehabilitate the author of *Betrachtungen* (published four years earlier) in the eyes of the men of the "new" age (it contains once more an explicit acknowledgment of his "conservative" book) but an appeal and an admonition directed to the nation's conscience. With an artist's sensitive reaction to the imponderable secondary currents of the *Zeitgeist,* he tried to shake out of its dangerous torpor the soul of a generation still undecided. He talked of "matters of humanity" and made it clear that he expected this subject to arouse opposition among the students. Nevertheless, he tried on this occasion to win over the recalcitrant with gently ironic, sometimes fiery and noble, persuasion, and, if need be, to beat them with their own weapons.

Mann pointed out how closely interwoven was the German romantic attitude to life (with special reference to that enigmatic genius Novalis) with the aspirations of the Enlightenment, democratic and humane in a profound and spiritual sense. He remained unperturbed by the commotion that spread through the audience when he talked of the "sterility of changeless conservatism" (he deliberately avoided the use of the word reaction) and of the "barbarism of insignificance" to which such an attitude led. Warningly he pointed to the mark of Cain in intellectual demoralization, to the "witless, uncouth and rowdy" behavior of a nationalist populace as contrasted with the "humanism, the mellow culture, the dignified and peaceful Germanism of the author of *The Weavers* [Gerhart Hauptmann]." He evoked Novalis's vision of a nobler and finer national statehood, in which everything temporal, local, and individual can be universalized. Indeed, universality had been the specific coloring of the early Romantic version of the national state, a coloring still in harmony with genuine, warm, and human feeling.

With all the strength of his heart and perceptive mind, Mann tried to exorcise the threatening danger:

Indeed, the sphere of the blood is in a terrible way also the sphere of bloodshed. It seems this is part of the coloring. War is romanticism. Nobody has ever denied the mystical, poetic element inherent in it. But today it is ludicrously bad romanticism, nauseatingly tainted poetry, and to deny that would be obduracy. If what is national is not to fall wholly into disrepute, if it is not to become solely a curse, then, instead of being the epitome of the old warlike, brawling spirit, it will have to become more and more completely the object of a cult of peace, thereby fulfilling its artistic and almost ecstatic nature.

And what was the answer of academic youth? Mann reported it in parenthese: "Shuffling of feet."* But he was not to be put off so easily by contradiction. Despite the mounting resistance from his audience, he again and again mobilized the full weight of his humanity and intellectual authority. The romantic spirit, under the spell of which he presumed his opponents to be, was, he protested, fatefully confused with obscurantism, "the political name of which is 'reaction.'" He repudiated the "sentimental barbarism," which so little deserved to be called Romanticism, a name for nobility and fineness of spirit, that the most confirmed romantic might well for the temporary emergency turn himself into a spokesman of political enlightenment. And the profound, visionary words of

---

*Among German students the shuffling of feet during an address is the traditional way of expressing dissent.—*Translators.*

Novalis, whose testimony Mann kept reinvoking, sound like a mockery of the fanatically reactionary student attitude at the time: "What does old mean? And young? Youth is where the future prevails. Age, where the past predominates."

In 1922 Walther Rathenau, the idealistic statesman of the German Republic, was murdered by a group of young Germans. Delivering this address at a time when this violent, senseless act still cast its oppressive shadow, Mann found words that should have inspired any young man or woman in whom the spiritual spark of goodness was not yet entirely extinct: "Young people and citizens, your opposition to the republic is a fear of words—you rear and shy at these words like restive horses; no sooner are these words pronounced than superstitious nervousness robs you of reason." However, there is a question that historical inquiry must not evade, the question, that is, of what political reality lay behind these persuasive words. Was the German Republic merely the stuff of dreams or was it reality? The following conditional clause of the author leaves room for doubt: "Democracy—as though this could not be more intimately homelike than some shining, saber-rattling and flaunting imperium!" No, the parliamentary compromise, the system of adjusting unadjustable tensions in a democratic state, was for them not "more intimately homelike."

For these young, obstinate enemies of democracy and of reason, which they despised, home was the dusky, mist-shrouded domain where sacrifices were offered to the gods of heroic rapture and national self-deification. Friedrich Hölderlin, Nietzsche, and George (to name only the most high-minded) were their tutelary genii, now being invoked against by a speaker from a different world, the world of clear thinking that was inimical to them. Was not democracy more apt to be a means, he suggested, to realize German beauty and a new humanism than the old powers of the state? He, too, the writer about the republic, certainly did not repudiate the traditional values, which indeed he had upheld in the self-confession of his *Betrachtungen*. And again he called on Novalis as a witness for the longed-for synthesis; the new must be grafted onto the stock and pith and develop beautiful forms. That was the task of a "German middle way" between Romanticism and Enlightenment, between mysticism and reason. Then as now, he said, he had, under immense pressure, endeavored to defend the element of humanism against Left and Right.

It was a tragic misjudgment. The past's clear voice, the voice of reason, was unable to penetrate to those stupefied and deluded by drunken lust for power. They lacked the "element of humanism." But even the rhapsodic Americanism chanted by Walt Whitman was incompatible with the new Romanticism of these young people. The fraternal call from the other side of the ocean had indeed found some response in a few sophisticated individuals, but not among the majority of a generation obsessed with nationalist defiance.

"To serve you, *ma femme*," the "thunderer from Manhattan" (Walt Whitman) had sung in his paean to Democracy. This must have raised a laugh with the adherents of *fehme* executions* and of reactionary conspiracies. Novalis as a romantic prophet of progress

*A *fehme* (or *vehme*) was the sentence decreed by a *Vehmgericht*, a medieval informally constituted tribunal that arrogated trial powers to itself. The Nazis had revived this infamous institution.—*Translators*.

and Whitman as a democratic romantic of human kindness! To these young nationalists such a view as Mann
held was nothing but the eccentric paradox of an overly
clever intellectual. They were barred once and for all
from the socialism of feelings proclaimed by Whitman:
"Would you have in yourself the divine, vast, general
law? Then merge yourself in it." They were locked out
by the national frontiers, that Marie von Ebner-Eschen-
bach, the humane Austrian novelist and aphorist, described as the barriers to love of one's neighbor.

To them the universal love of Whitman, "of the
son of Manhattan," a love which compassionately em-
braced the whole of mankind, not in Christian humility
but from sheer exuberant vitality, meant nothing.
Neither the language of Whitman nor of Novalis could
penetrate their "inner realm." To these young nationalists, the heroes of the Nibelungen saga, that barbaric
myth of treachery, malice, and the "heroism of violence," were better understood and fitted more readily
into the picture of the world painted by their demagogues, distorted as it was by fantasies of a war of
revenge. It was unavailing to point out to them that a
"knight of the blue flower" (Novalis) had called for a
law of nations as a beginning of universal legislation.
Not for them was this kind of Romanticism that was
politically enlightened enough to proclaim: "National
states must learn at long last that the achievement of all
their aims is possible only through universal action"
(this "at long last" was said by Novalis around 1800!).

Goethe, Novalis, Whitman, Mann, and Hauptmann—these were not their men, and the shuffling of
feet continued. All right then—as Mann tried to per-
suade them (and himself)—so we shall not shrink from
laying bare for these young men the concrete roots of

all the pale humanist ideas, that is to say, love, in the original close-to-nature sense of the word. It was love, Mann told them, that united the minds of two continents and two eras, that linked the "voluptuous thinker of dreams" of the Old World and the mighty panerotic poet of the New. As a third witness he finally called upon Goethe's *Wilhelm Meister*, to speak for the humanism of sensual beauty as experienced by the individual. The indivisible unity of the beauty of body and soul that belonged to classical Hellenism, had not this been reborn out of the spirit of American democracy?

On the basis of this erotic-spiritual conception of democracy, Mann boldly took the wind out of the nationalists' sails, spoke of a "third realm of religious humanism," in which the due of Eros was, not indeed the crown—that would be "medievalism and the spirit of chivalry"—but the highest republican and democratic honors and titles. A political dream vision, a utopia of the most attractive and daring kind, was conjured up in striking fashion, yet with the utmost sensitiveness: ". . . it would please Walt Whitman if we were to confer upon the young god [Eros] the presidency of this new realm."

During that same year, 1922, the year Rathenau was murdered, Moeller van den Bruck's *Das dritte Reich* [The Third Reich] was published. (It was he who provided the label "Third Reich" for the era of Hitler's rule.) It contained the only self-criticism of German nationalism, for which reason the National Socialists repudiated him with loud protests. He had, after all, been bold enough to point out that it was impossible to make sense of this "philosophical" conception of the German third realm, or "Third Reich." "Strangely cloudy, sentimental and evanescent, and altogether otherworldly" were the words van den Bruck used to describe the notions that the Germans associated with the term "Third Reich." "The German people," he wrote in his preface, "are only too prone to delusions. The idea of the Third Reich could turn out to be the greatest delusion in which they ever indulged."

Mann was one of the few who warned of the preposterous, vicious, and false function of eroticism in the circles of the *"fehme"* and the young frustrated "heroes." He described the dark and sinister fusion of erotic ties and military discipline, for which there exist only a few valid literary testimonies, such as M. R. Hesse's novel about a Reichswehr officer, *Partenau* (1929), or P. M. Lampel's documentary novel *Verratene Jungen* [Betrayed Boys]. Mann's explanation of the obscure motives underlying dashing attitudes makes plain even to the most biased reader the meaning of the "connection between disease, death, and desire" that so often recurs as a leitmotiv in his narrative and reflective prose. The pathologically cruel aspects of barracks-room communities, and the sadistic, homosexual, though hindered, libido common among them were, similarly, exposed in the personal reminiscences published by the sociologist Leopold von Wiese and by Ernst von Salomon, the accomplice of Rathenau's murderers, both authors having been Prussian cadets in their youth.

The romantic interpretation of life as a malady, an interpretation intimately familiar to Novalis and not alien, either, to Whitman, the patriarch of American, freedom-loving vitality, was nowhere better exemplified than by the perverted instincts of Prussianism. To follow up these interconnections is to uncover the reasons why the poetic summons to humanism (a concept described by Mann as "a little old-fashioned and always bright once more with the glamor of youth") aroused no response among the obstinate youthful victims of the demagogues. The great mass of First World War veterans, boastfully claiming they had never been defeated, was deaf and impervious to the clarifying, awaking voice of reason. It needed the roll of a new drummer of violence to carry them away—to a new march to death.

But the fundamental feature of Mann's discursive prose is not really polemics in the strict sense, is not a debate conducted in passionate terms, but rather, and to an outstanding degree, a psychological and critical testing, a dissection of slogans embodying the passions of the day. Before the storm broke, during the last years of external calm, when life was still comfortable and enjoyable, and probably before he knew anything of Freud's methods, Mann, in the essay *Der alte Fontane* (*The Old Fontane*), published in 1910, wrote these words: "Psychology is the sharpest sapping tool of enlightenment." He demonstrated the psychological novelist's "disintegrating" function, which inescapably makes him a social critic, by the example of Theodor Fontane, who in his mature manhood extrolled the myth of the old Prussian nobility and, when old age had sharpened his powers of skeptical observation, dropped pacifist and antimilitarist remarks in his letters and reviews.

Psychology, not as some sort of theoretical method but in the sense of the novelist's keen observation, is the skeptical technique Mann used in order to look below the surface, in the political no less than in the social and cultural sphere. And below the surface he invariably discovered the plastic reality of human character.

Man was his yardstick for the effectiveness of human ideas, man was for him the measure of things, and man the example by which he demonstrated the influence of thought.

In this perspective Mann's commentaries on the "spirit of the age" turn into psychological and character studies of men in their time. Figures such as Ibsen, Gerhart Hauptmann, John Galsworthy, Jakob Wassermann, Hugo von Hofmannsthal, and Knut Hamsun were for Mann not "interesting" subjects for literary portraits but an opportunity for discussions dealing with the history of ideas and cultural criticism. Oswald Spengler, for instance, is characterized with superb shrewdness as the author of an "intellectual novel," a "defeatist of humanity," an "anti-intellectual snob" and, finally, as the "true son and last talent of materialist civilization."

Charlatans, too, are unmasked entirely by precise literary portraiture. In his essay *Okkulte Erlebnisse (An Experience in the Occult)* Mann proved the absurdity of the pseudoscientific, rigged-up hocus-pocus of the occultist Schrenck-Notzing not by theoretical refutation, but by the feigned "positive skepticism" of the subtly ironic description of a séance. This literary record of rather shady practices belongs to the feverish atmosphere of the period of inflation and thus comes within the sphere of *The Magic Mountain*, which, though concluding with the First World War, encompasses certain elements of the postwar years.

The occult theme recurs in *Mario und der Zauberer (Mario and the Magician),* a novella that Mann described as an improvisation alongside the critical preparatory work for his "main business," that is—from the end of the 1920s—the first volume of the Joseph tetralogy. With his customary precision in the description of details, Mann here recounts a rather repulsive and depressing occurrence. By hypnotism, a show-booth conjurer subjects a young Italian waiter to public humiliation. The episode goes back to one of Mann's trips to Italy, and it is not quite clear whether, in telling it, he intended an allusion to the Fascist regime's practices of trapping souls by force and fraud. The novella is mentioned in *A Sketch of My Life,* but without reference to any political meaning. The relevant passage, on the other hand, is very instructive about Mann's working technique, which always had room for impromptu ideas. For that reason it is reproduced here.

Since I am no good at "resting" with no work in hand and find on the whole it does me more harm than good, I decided to fill my mornings with an easy task, the working out of an anecdote for which I got the idea from an earlier holiday trip, a stay at Forte dei Marmi near Viareggio; it would be a piece of work that required no paraphernalia and which, in the most effortless sense of the word, could be "pulled out of thin air." I began to write in my room during the morning hours, as I was used to doing, but missing the sea made me restless and I did not seem to be getting on. I did not think working outdoors would be any good. I need to have a roof over my head, to prevent my thoughts evaporating in dreams. It was a difficult dilemma. Only the sea could have brought it about, and fortunately it turned out that the sea, by its peculiar nature, was also able to remove it. I allowed myself to be persuaded to take my writing down to the beach. I moved my wicker chair quite close to the water, which was full of bathers. Like that, scribbling on my knees, before me the wide horizon which kept being intersected by people walking by, surrounded by a happy crowd, visited by naked children snatching at my pencils, I let it happen. Unexpectedly, my anecdote grew into a fable, the loose telling of a story into an organized tale, a private experience into something symbolic of a moral—while all along I was filled with a happy astonishment at the sea's capacity to absorb all human disturbances and dissolve them in its loved immensity.

"Improvisation" is doubtless also the right way to describe the novella *Unordnung und frühes Leid (Disorder and Early Sorrow)*. It, too, was written between two pieces of "main business," work on *The Magic Mountain* and on the Joseph tetralogy. In it the author commemorates a domestic interlude with intense pleasure. The story is almost openly autobiographical in character. A tender and solicitous father confesses to some "disorder" in his family and domestic affairs, a symbolic disorder which expresses the slackening of relationships between parents and children after the First World War. Mann described this novella as gay; he indulgently goes along with the disorder, but there is a sad undertone. Mann was a kind and understanding father, though quite unlike the traditional idea of a patriarchal head of the family. No doubt he took the same view of educational matters as Goethe, who once said: "We cannot shape children after our wishes."

Mann's six children, three sons and three daughters, looked upon their father as a paragon; they called him the "magician." But much as they adored their famous father, they clearly felt a little overshadowed by him. This was especially true of the older children, and quite particularly of the highly gifted Klaus, for whom the great name was often a burden. He committed suicide on May 22, 1949 in Cannes. Apart from him, the oldest daughter, Erika, and the youngest son, Michael, were gifted artists. Erika Mann was an actress and made a name in cabaret satire, and during the Second World War she traveled all over the world as a foreign correspondent. Michael Mann is a violinist. The second son, Golo, has made a reputation for himself as a historian.

One of the duties as a public figure that Thomas Mann undertook with pleasure was to give lectures abroad during the years of the Weimar Republic. He was welcomed wherever he went and often honored by outstanding men of letters and politics; he made lecture tours in the Netherlands, Switzerland, Denmark, England, Spain, France, and Poland.

His own, rather optimistic, view of Europe was that the war had made it "as it were, smaller, more compact, and more intimate." In the official language, which politely glossed over persistent contradictions, Mann was "the object of the most emphatic manifestations in the service of cultural reconciliation."

In the diary of his French trip, which was published in 1926 under the title *Pariser Rechenschaft* [Account of My Stay in Paris], Mann recalls the slightly comic aspects of a ceremonial reception in the grand style. But he was flattered enough at being assigned the part of "ambassador extraordinary of German culture." Henri Lichtenberger, the Germanist, expressed the spirit of the occasion by quoting Nietzsche: "Words and sounds are rainbows and dream bridges linking what is eternally divided."

In his reply Mann dissociated himself from the sort of embarrassing, false warmth of which Germans like to boast, and instead professed the "civilized satisfactions" of sympathy and mutual understanding. (Aristide Briand, the great foreign minister of France, no doubt had the same thing in mind when he spoke of *"rapprochement."*) With reference to the idea of a reconciled Europe, Mann used the fine phrase "Child of Eros and reason, by another name called goodness."

But he knew very well that he could not claim to speak for the whole of intellectual Germany. The mind was neutralized in Germany, he told his Paris friends, and German writers were "a bit like stylites."

In 1929, Mann received the Nobel Prize for Literature. The Swedish Academy's statement of award made it clear that the honor was intended primarily for the author of *Buddenbrooks,* the "Nordic" character of which made it particularly attractive to Scandinavians. Mann's reaction to this high distinction was that of a man self-confident indeed but by no means self-satisfied, a man who felt that he was called upon to maintain his status and fill a dignified role. In *A Sketch of My Life* he remarked:

It [the distinction] was no doubt bound to come my way—I say it without presumption, from a detached though not disinterested understanding of the character of my destiny, of my "role" on earth, a role of which the dubious glitter of success is part and parcel and which I look upon simply in human terms, without making much intellectual fuss about it. In such a mood of thoughtfully receptive detachment I acknowledged the clamorous episode, an occasion for much celebration and kindness to me, as fittingly belonging to my life, and got through it with the best bearing I could—inner bearing, too, which is more difficult.

The Nobel Prize had been preceded a few years earlier by the award of an honorary degree by the University of Bonn, an unusual honor for a writer. *Tempora mutantur*—in 1937, after Adolf Hitler had deprived him of his citizenship, the university withdrew

the honorary title from Mann. By that time, Mann was
in exile; his reply to the dean of the faculty of philosophy at Bonn University in a letter that revealed
his hurt feelings and indignation, contains words
which, as it were, write finis to his role as a representative German: "I sought to prevent, with my lim-
ited powers, something that was wrong, and thereby
I conjured up the fate with which I must now come
to terms, a fate essentially alien to my nature but with
which I must learn to live."

This sentence is doubly and profoundly significant
insofar as it alludes at the same time to the fate of the
great mythical figure which preoccupied Mann during the greater part of his exile, that is, Joseph, the
erstwhile spoiled favorite of his father, who was cast
out by his brethren and sold into an alien country.
Planned originally as a novella, "a wing of a historical
triptych," this many-faceted work, widely ramified
and penetrating into the beginnings of recorded time,
was to become the spiritual companion of Mann in
foreign lands.

8

Myth
and
Psychology

In his essay on Fontane, already mentioned, the Brandenburg Huguenot and liberal Prussian, Mann wrote, "Psychology is the sharpest sapping tool of enlightenment."

The fact that he took a biblical subject from the Old Testament, which preoccupied him for more than a decade—it accounted for the bulk of his work from 1927 to the end of 1942—was later often interpreted as a departure from psychological realism. But what Mann wrote in *A Sketch of My Life* in 1930, shortly after he began working on the Joseph tetralogy, makes it irrefutably clear that there is an underlying conception of humanism and enlightenment in this monumental work of more than two thousand pages. What first attracted Mann to the Genesis story was a series of pictures by which a painter friend of the family, whom Mrs. Mann had known since her youth, illustrated the Joseph legend.

Then Mann happened upon a sentence in Goethe's *Dichtung und Wahrheit,* which said: "This human story is most charming, but it seems too short, and it is tempting to develop it in detail." Goethe's words were the decisive impulse and, as Mann tells us, they became the motto of his working life for years to come. The task of retelling and remaking a story reaching back to the frontiers of prehistorical time had its attractions. As Mann declared: "There was for me an indescribable sensuous as well as intellectual fascination in writing a novel penetrating so deeply into the roots of humanity instead of the customary setting of modern, bourgeois life." But almost in the same breath he also gave a clear indication of a second motivation for his undertaking, namely, the scientific curiosity of a man seeking, by means constantly subject to rational counterchecks, to gain knowledge of the origins of the human condition from the condition of primitive man.

In *A Sketch of My Life*, again, the author revealed the basic personal and generally human reason for "looking back":

The advances of science both into the darkness of pre-history and into the night of the unconscious by investigations that at a certain point meet and coincide, have vastly extended the range of anthropological knowledge back into the depths of time, or, what really comes to the same thing, down into the depths of the soul, and in all of us there is an active curiosity about the earliest and oldest human matters, about what lies before reason, about myth and the history of religion.

Thomas Mann's intention to apply psychology to myth is revealed equally clearly in a letter he wrote in 1941, nearly at the end of his vast achievement, to his adviser, the Hungarian historian of religion and myth, K. Kerényi: "What indeed should be my concern right now except myth plus psychology. I have long been passionately interested in this combination. It fore-shadows the world of the future, a humanity blessed with the blessings of the spirit above and of the deep that lieth under."

With the impetus of scientific thoroughness, going back to sources accessible only to intensive research, Mann, scholarly writer and poetic scholar that he was, approached a task still far from solution, the task, that is, of releasing myth from the reservations fenced in by the taboos of blind forces of faith.

A bold and new exegesis was the result of Mann's going back to the mysterious revelations of the beginning and exploring them gently and persistently. He deciphered the symbolic language of the Bible and re-

vealed in its images the slow process of man's becoming
conscious of himself. In addition, he placed the biblical
images into their setting of historical facts as ascer-
tained by scientific research. This is how the Joseph
tetralogy, going far beyond his original conception,
ended, even more than *The Magic Mountain,* as a classical and at the same time eminently modern *Bildungsroman.*

While the first part, *Die Geschichten Jaakobs (The
Tales of Jacob),* still has the magic charm of mythical
poetry, the later volumes with their description of
Joseph's life show how the dreamer turns into a man
of knowledge.

The dreamlike vagueness of Joseph's thought acquires the increasingly sharp outline of knowledge. He
develops into a personality by releasing the conscious
ego from the mythical darkness of collectivity. To acquire consciousness is tantamount to maturity for
Mann, in line with modern depth psychology, which
leaves its imprint on the very intonation and accent of
his language. By his mythical destinies and adventures
Joseph grows out of the patriarchal idyll of a favorite
son, out of a naïve, narcissistic self-admiration and
imagined godlike state to mastery of his fate, turns
into a mature human being fulfilling his "role" with
subtle humor and ironic self-detachment. Like Hans
Castorp in *The Magic Mountain,* the "prodigy" Joseph
is a problem child of life. In his dreams of godlikeness
he resembles the primordial type of artist, whose social
and metaphysical special position preoccupied Mann
throughout his life. To this extent Joseph is an imago,
a secret wish fulfillment of his "modern" narrator and
exploiter.

Historians of literature have tried to discover in

Mann's figure of Joseph certain analogies and allusions linking up with the history of religion and with mythology. For the main features, the author stuck to Genesis. But he added a liberal sprinkling of more or less concealed comparisons with other cults of antiquity. The "primordial images" of Osiris, Adonis, Tammuz, and Dionysus are perceptible in the background, and in the mythical frame of reference in which the author places the figure of Joseph himself, the latter is even seen as a precursor of Jesus. There are primordial types and "archetypes" as outlined by C. G. Jung. But the "timeless" figures of the novel nevertheless stand in their correct temporal setting.

In the course of extensive study trips to Egypt and Palestine Mann familiarized himself with the monuments of the Middle East's ancient civilizations. He applied an often pedantic exactitude and thoroughness to furnishing the period background with graphic and picturesque detail. Any reader prepared to follow the images of the novel patiently will find that it conjures up a close-at-hand view of the spare landscape of the old Israelitic herdsmen, that he shares the pastoral idylls of Jacob's loves and marriages and his paternal cares, and that the luxuriant panorama of the rich Egyptian civilization unfolds before his eyes more clearly than in any museum.

The Joseph novels, especially the later ones, *Joseph in Agypten* (*Joseph in Egypt*) and *Joseph der Ernährer* (*Joseph the Provider*), relativize the myth by transposing it into a realistic life story, into a real, historically verified social world and system of government. However much Joseph's experiences and conflicts may symbolize basic human situations, they

are nevertheless linked to historical events, such as the
fratricidal wars of the Israelites, emigration, exposure,
imprisonment, the cunning rise to power of some slave
owner's favorite. And history in the grand style is mani-
fest in Joseph's encounter with Pharaoh Amenophis IV,
called Akhenaton (c. 1370 B.C.), whose likeness as a
worshiper of the sun has been preserved in several ef-
figies. Mann represented the husband of the lovely
Nefertiti as a young man refined to the point of decadence, a convinced monotheist, a tolerant and ecstatic
admirer of the arts who applied himself most reluct-
antly to wearisome affairs of state.

In the magnificent dialogue between Joseph and
Akhenaton, the pharaoh proves an "enlightened," indeed revolutionary modernist in contrast to the realistic, conservative son of the "shepherd king." The
words that Mann, using free association over relativ-
ized time, puts in his pharaoh's mouth would have done
credit to the young Goethe in his pantheistic mood.

More than that, this dialogue between a boy-king
weary of barbarism and the young, "practical" Jewish
social moralist and political prophet is almost Faustian
in character over long stretches. Joseph says: "For God
is the whole," and the pharaoh replies: "He is the light
and the sweet disk of the sun, whose rays embrace the
lands and bind them with love, and only the wicked,
whose faith is turned downward, have strong hands."
And in the following sentences we recognize the voice
of a man of insight and love, who associatively antici-
pates the dreadful experiences of subsequent millennia:

Believe me, men are a helpless race. They cannot do
anything on their own; by themselves they never think
of the slightest new idea. All they do is imitate the gods,

and they act according to the image they have of the gods. Purify the deity, and you will purify man.

That is a timeless confession, an associative anachronism, by which Akhenaton's possible visions are linked up with the knowledge of the twentieth-century novelist who, being no longer "bound," is at bottom no longer religious. Strictly speaking, it is a denial of mythos within a myth.

It should be remembered that the last volume of the Joseph tetralogy (*Joseph the Provider*) was published in Stockholm in 1943, the year of the surrender of the Germans at Stalingrad.

It was a strange road that led the author of the demythologized legend of mankind from the intellectual expedition he had planned when safely at home, to the adventure of having to confront his inner vision with the horrors of actual events. Now a writer of another Germany, in exile, he found confirmation of what he had had in mind at the beginning of his mighty epic, when, with reference to the Joseph legend, he wrote in *A Sketch of My Life*:

The spell increased. Much of its strength derived from the idea of integration, succession, continuity, of carrying on the work on a human theme handed down by tradition, an idea which likewise at my age gains power of attraction. The material was an ancient cultural heritage, a heritage of the imagination, too, a favorite subject of all the arts, treated scores of times in the East and West in art and literature. My work, whether good or bad, would find its historical place in this sequence and tradition, bearing the imprint of its hour and region.

9

The

Writer

in Exile

" . . . **F**or I love order as part of nature and as a deeply lawful instinct, as the silent destiny and the befitting clarity of a productive plan of life." In this sentence Mann gave a provisional account of himself.

The intellectual spokesman of the Weimar Republic, who had described his receipt of the Nobel Prize for Literature as an episode, an honor no doubt bound to come his way, wished, as a writer and citizen, to be governed by a rational and humane principle of order. He believed he could combine the incompatible, be demoniacal and official at the same time. He was a founding member of the Section of Letters in the Prussian Academy of Arts, evaded no honor and no representative obligation proposed to him. His daily round of work, three hours in the morning at his desk, then reading and correspondence, family and friends—all that added up to the "claims of the day" that he conscientiously tried to meet.

What was "metaphysical and individual" in him he felt to be diametrically opposed to the "social" claims, to which he submitted "after violent struggles." The tension between adventures of the mind and civic duties became the secret spice of life for the aging family man and prosperous burgher.

In the speech that he delivered in 1925 on the occasion of the 700th anniversary of his native city Lübeck, he confessed to a sublimated concept of the patrician civic spirit. He said:

"Ethics" is opposed to mere aesthetics, to reveling in beauty and pleasure, as well as to nihilism and the vagabondage of death. It is ethics that really makes a man *a citizen of life* [Mann's italics], the sense of duty without which there can be no impulse for achievement, for any productive contribution to life and development. It is this that impels an artist not to conceive of art as an absolute exemption from human affairs, makes him found a home and family, and provide his intellectual life, which may often be adventurous enough, with a solid, worthy—I can again find only the word bourgeois—foundation. If I have acted and lived in that style, there can be no doubt at all that one of the determining reasons was my father's example.

To fulfill his representative role gave Mann concern rather than satisfaction. The ambiguous aura of success, later of fame, burdened his external life with claims to which he hardly felt equal any more. Writing in 1930, he paid a grateful tribute, therefore, to his wife, who by that time had shared his life for twenty-five years, "an onerous life, requiring patience more than anything else, and easily subject to weariness and distraction."

Honored and feted, surrounded by people who wanted help or advice, fostering young talents, patient and often all too indulgent, he did not know that the heaviest burden was yet to come. Thomas Mann certainly recognized the signs of crisis, but he did not realize that the catastrophe was so near at hand. He was facing the uncertainties of the coming era with a secure sense of his vocation. The year 1932, when the centenary of Goethe's death was commemorated with pompous celebrations, was the year which brought the turning point, when the scales were tipped in favor of the mindless and power-hungry forces intent on destroying Germany's humanistic cultural tradition.

Mann was one of the speakers at the Weimar Goethe celebrations in March 1932. His two great commemorative speeches, *Goethe als Repräsentant des bürgerlichen Zeitalters* (*Goethe as Representative of the*

Bourgeois Age) and *Goethes Laufbahn als Schriftsteller* (*Goethe's Career as a Man of Letters*) were in-
cluded as the first two items in the last volume of
Mann's essays to be published in prewar Germany,
entitled *Leiden und Größe der Meister* [Suffering and
Greatness of the Masters]. Mann was perhaps one of
the last Germans who could say of himself, quite natu-
rally and without presumption: "I am no Goethe, but I
do belong a little to his family." This intimacy was
entirely due to Mann's still keeping alive his attach-
ment to the concept of fine humanity that Goethe had
given the Germans. Mann's endeavors to liberate the
image of Goethe from the rigidity of a dead, cultural
ideal, aimed in the first place at setting aside the barriers of blind idolatry and approaching the great "man
inside the poet" without priestly ceremony. He looked
for the human being behind the spurious legend. Even
Goethe, worshipped as "Olympian" by the cultural
philistines, was a man of his age, and Mann did not
hesitate to look upon him as an outstanding bourgeois.

Universal humanity rooted in respectable bourgeois life,
world stature as a child of the bourgeoisie—such a destiny,
in its origins and audacious growth, is nowhere as much
at home as with us, and everything German that has
grown from the bourgeois world into the world of the
spirit has a smiling home in the house of the Frankfurt
burgher.

But Mann's rational or, as one is tempted to say,
reverently sober interpretation of Goethe reveals also
the weakness of the bourgeois attitude to life. He calls
Goethe a "thoroughly German nonpatriot" in contrast
to Schiller, the "patriot of mankind with a humanitar-
ian, revolutionary spirit," to which the French literary
spirit had stood godfather. Goethe's outlook was intel-

lectual, cultural, cosmopolitan, and opposed to the French Revolution, not because it extended human frontiers but because it doctrinarily narrowed them. Goethe acknowledged no political and revolutionary ideas; "he was a fighter and liberator in the sphere of morality and the mind, and especially in erotic matters, but not in state and civic affairs." What the descendants of the classical cultural tradition regard as a moderate, skeptical attitude in Goethe, appeared to many of his contemporaries, including some of his admirers and worshipers, as a tendency to negation, a profound irony with respect to all things human. Among the bourgeois speakers of the 1932 celebrations, Mann was probably the only one not to overlook the dualism in Goethe, the sediment of antisocial individualism which the revolutionaries resented so much in the Weimar statesman. Yet the unique example of the great poet is a lesson in resignation flowing from the self-conquest of the spirit of skeptical negation.

This is how Mann interpreted *Wilhelm Meister,* the novel in which the aged Goethe foresaw the social and technological development of the century: "The ideal of the private individual as a universal man is dropped and the age of the specialist is proclaimed. There is the feeling, still dominant today, of the individual's insufficiency. Perfect humanity needs all men, the individual becomes a function, the idea of community comes to the force; and the Jesuitical, military spirit of the pedagogic province, leavened by the arts as it is, allows hardly anything to survive from the individualist and liberal, bourgeois ideal." It may be that Mann's interpretation of *Wilhelm Meister's Wanderjahre* as a sublime, forward-looking attempt to resolve the tension between individual and community in an "imperialism of love" was merely a hypothesis of loving tribute, for the broad prospect of Goethe's polymorphic view of the world and his intellectual landscape led the twentieth-century novelist to a vision in which Tolstoy's world combines with Western humanism in a classless society of the future.

Mann rejected such distorted views as are implied in the allegedly insoluble conflict between "bourgeois humanism and socialist salvation." In an epilogue to the Goethe year, published in the review *Der Querschnitt*, he wrote:

Were those public speakers right who would have had us refrain from celebrating him, because we were unworthy of him and because his spirit, his synthesis, were remote from today's reality and alien to it? That this is so is confirmed by those who seek to wrest Germany away from the community of nations, who demand that Germany should forgo the world's sympathy and understanding, should defiantly withdraw into the jungle of savage dynamic forces, of amorphous strength and nature; but is this the intent, the true character of that noble identity whose name is Germany?

While this reproachful question is addressed to German nationalism, there is an undertone of regret that Goethe's name was no longer a bond for the whole nation and all classes. Once before Mann had called for a synthesis, had transcended space and time to fuse Latin civilization with primitive, vital faith in the future. This was in his great essay on Goethe and Tolstoy, where he tried to find in the spirit of Rousseau, whom he loved, a common denominator for the classical spokesman of the East and the great German. There are hints of strange and yet profoundly symbolic influences exercised by the age of Enlightenment. ". . . The striving of the spirit's sons toward nature, and of nature's children toward the spirit"—this, for Mann, is the way leading to a humanity beyond all conflicts.

Europe's good angels, humanism and enlightenment, have handed down a tradition of desire for liberty tempered by ironic reservations, and it is this which the interpreter of Goethe's and Tolstoy's brand of humanity praised as the "appeal of the middle way." German reality and German dreams interwove in Thomas Mann in a conception that was bound to founder on the hard, political realities. That is why the Promised Land implied in his invocation of Goethe's name on the eve of the German disaster sounds so utopian.

When Hitler came to power, Mann was working on an essay entitled *Leiden und Größe Richard Wagners* (*The Sufferings and Greatness of Richard Wagner*). It sounds like one of Fate's bad jokes that the uncivilized and brutal man of violence who gave the Weimar republic its death blow was as much an admirer of Wagner's music as the Weimar republic's representative writer. But Hitler would have found little to please him in Mann's interpretation of the master's work, for the author did not pass over in silence the dangerous and dubious aspects of the composer's nature.

While the Reichstag was burning in Berlin, Mann and his wife Katja were on a lecture tour. He had spoken on the theme of the Wagner essay in Brussels, Amsterdam, Paris, and other cities abroad and, as planned, was having a holiday at Arosa when he got a warning telephone call from Munich, where his eldest children Klaus and Erika were getting ready to flee.

This was in the early days of March 1933. Thomas

Mann stayed on in Switzerland. Not until many years later was he to see his once beautiful house in Munich again, reduced to ruins by bombs.

Thomas Mann and his family were not forced into exile—it was self-imposed. The Third Reich might not have borne down upon them too implacably. The state might have wished to keep the world-famous name at home. At first, a blind eye was turned on Mrs. Mann's "non-Aryan" birth. There was no lack of attempts to make the family change their mind. To be sure, Erika Mann had run the left-wing, satirical cabaret *Die Pfeffermühle* [The Pepper Mill] at Munich, and Klaus Mann had taken a risk as an opponent of the German nationalists, but there were plenty of friends who tried to smooth things over.

Klaus Mann, the fitful genius among the author's sons, and the oldest of them, spoke for the whole family when, in *Der Wendepunkt* [The Turning Point], a book of memoirs of touching sincerity, he wrote:

Were we, then, "voluntary" exiles? Not quite. We could not go back. We would have died of disgust, disgust at our own wretchedness and at the vile behavior around us. To some lungs the air of the Third Reich was unbreathable. We would have suffocated at home.

Klaus Mann spoke not merely for himself and his family. Many of the best German writers, and not only those persecuted for "racial" reasons, left Hitler's Germany as Thomas and Heinrich Mann did.

These literary exiles did more for Germany than the disunited political ones with all their party factions. The writers in exile upheld the dignity of the German intellectual tradition more visibly and resolutely than did the secret resistance of the anti-Hitler opposition in

Germany itself. One of their chief self-imposed tasks was to maintain the contacts between German and world literature. In Amsterdam, Klaus Mann, supported by his friends, became editor of the international literary review *Die Sammlung*. His sister Erika attacked the Nazi crimes from Zurich, through another political cabaret, again called "The Pepper Mill."

Mann refrained from polemical utterances during the first years of his exile. His works, though declared undesirable, were still sold in Germany. When he sided more and more openly with the victims of persecution, the Nazi rulers turned their wrath upon him, too. In 1936 he was first deprived of his citizenship and soon afterward of his honorary doctorate. This latter move hurt him deeply and induced him to write a letter of protest that aroused attention throughout the world. The author of *Buddenbrooks* and his entire family, his sons Golo and Michael, his daughters Monika and Elizabeth, were declared to have forfeited their German nationality. (Klaus and Erika Mann had already been deprived of their citizenship.)

From this moment (1936) onward, Thomas Mann was the foremost representative of the "other" Germany, a role forced upon him by fate and implying, to a far greater degree than at home, an obligation to speak up in public and step out from the quiet seclusion of his study.

It was due only to the strictest discipline and an unswervingly conscientious devotion to his work that this hatred of Nazi barbarity and his understandable bitterness about his destiny did not seriously interrupt progress with the great epic novel he then had in hand, and that the grand, consistent design of the work remained unimpaired.

Mann's study at Küsnacht, near Zurich, which
Klaus Mann showed me during a visit to Switzerland
in 1938, when Thomas Mann was in the United States,
was like a symbol of continuity and permanence. The
family had managed to get a few pieces of their Munich furniture out of the country: the Biedermeier
bookcases from Lübeck that sheltered behind glass
doors the Sophien edition of Goethe's works in its gilt
leather binding; a few pictures, including Lenbach's
portrait of the young Katja Mann as a page, as well as
a painting by Ludwig von Hofmann depicting three
young men posed like statuary beside a lake in standing or reclining positions; an Egyptian bust; and,
finally, the desk at which he worked so steadily in
writing the Joseph tetralogy—at first in Munich, then
in Zurich, and completed in California. Tidily ar-
ranged on the desk were his writing implements and
the framed photographs of the youngest children; the
refined and comfortably conservative atmosphere of a
bourgeois home was preserved, and it was more than
decorum.

During Mann's first trip to the United States, when
he was traveling on one of the comfortable liners, he
found time to read *Don Quixote*. His essay on Cer-
vantes is the final one in the volume *Leiden und Größe
der Meister*. *Meerfahrt mit Don Quijote* (*Voyage with
Don Quixote*) is the title of the melancholy essay in
which the famous outlaw discusses the problem of
exile.

The reflections of the banished author of *Voyage
with Don Quixote* contain some sentences which throw
a particularly clear light on his political stand and his
metaphysical views of history. These sentences explain
the "anti-Germanism" forced upon him by current

events and at the same time testify to his German humanism:

Self-irony, freedom, and artistically easygoing self-indulgence may not make a nation particularly efficient in the context of history, but they are attractive qualities, and ultimately the balance of attractive and repulsive qualities does count in history. Whatever the historical pessimists maintain, human beings have a conscience, even if it be only an aesthetic one, a conscience of taste. True, they bow to success, to the *fait accompli* of power, regardless of how it came about. But at heart they do not forget the humanly ugly things, the violent injustice and brutality that have taken place in their midst, and without their sympathy no success of power and efficiency is tenable in the long run.

Thomas Mann saw the positive protagonists of humanity and liberalism not in the skeptical, ironical, and artistically easygoing product of Latin civilizations, but in the German world citizen Goethe, who became the lodestar of the two most important works written by Mann during his American exile, the novels *Lotte in Weimar (The Beloved Returns: Lotte in Weimar)* and *Doktor Faustus (Doctor Faustus).*

More so than in any of his earlier works Mann was here closely concerned with the German past, at its heights and depths, in *Lotte in Weimar* with classical Weimar and, finally, in bold confrontation with Hitler's Germany, with the late Middle Ages and the early Reformation. The book built around Goethe is a symbol of glamor and depth, and perhaps the finest of all realistic visions of Goethe. The great figure through whom Germany once, and maybe for the only time, inspired the whole world with love and ungrudging admiration, is released in Mann's novel from the pedestal on which the schoolmasters have put him, and thus seems delightfully close to us. Although Mann studied the source material as industriously as any professor of German literature, he relegated all the philological drudgery to the background. Unlike many of his predecessors among Goethe scholars, he had the courage to approach the sacral with reverence, certainly, but also with a little irony. He overturned the statue and found Goethe the man, in all his greatness and weakness.

Mann was not afraid to describe how much all those who loved Goethe and served him unselfishly had to suffer. But he also gave an interpretation of the sacrifice involved in their love and resignation. The ghostlike conversation between Goethe and Lotte in her old age epitomizes Goethe's existence in a formulation more noble and beautiful than most. During their drive in the carriage together, which is so described that the reader is left uncertain whether it actually happens or whether Lotte merely dreams it, Mann allows Goethe to meditate thus:

"Dear soul, let me answer you most sincerely, in farewell and reconciliation. You speak of sacrifice, but there's a mystery about that and a great unity as there is with the world, with life, with a person and his work, and change is everything. We sacrificed to the gods, and in the end it was the god who was the sacrifice. You used a symbol that is dear to me and akin like no other, and my soul has been obsessed with it as long as I can think: that of the moth and the lethal attraction of the flame. You would have me be the flame into which the moth greedily plunges, but then, in the change and exchange of things I am also the burning candle, which sacrifices its body so that the light may glow, and again, I am also the butterfly consumed by the flame—a symbol of every sacrifice of life and body in spiritual transformation. Dear soul, old and childlike soul, I am first and last a sacrifice—and he who offers it. Once I burned for you, and I burn for you at all times to spirit and light."

As a successor to Goethe, Mann is occasionally led to identify himself so strongly with the poet's manner of speech that actual quotations often fuse strangely with the style the author of *Buddenbrooks* used in his old age. Yet we should think twice before we apply the term Alexandrian to this elaborately parodistical but nevertheless individual artistry of language. As Mann himself stressed more than once, the *imitatio* of Goethe was just another device for getting himself into the appropriate mood for writing, the mental attitude he needed for the literary objectivization of his reckoning with the inhumane powers of Germany. In this sense *Lotte in Weimar* is, so far as the artistry of its language is concerned, a prelude to *Doctor Faustus,* that work of hatred and cheated love, which is as problematical as it is rich in problems. In the novel about Lotte, Mann faced man's weakness as an ingredient of his greatness; what is revealed in the life story of the composer Adrian Leverkühn, is man's frailty sublimated in a work of art. A fitting motto for *Doctor Faustus* might be found in Goethe's words from *Iphigenie:* "All human frailty is redeemed by pure humanity."

The novelist grew old in exile; he was disillusioned and—rightly so—embittered, less perhaps about his own destiny than about his nation's regression into barbarism. He was gripped by a feeling that death was near. While he was writing *Doctor Faustus*, a dangerous illness, which necessitated a lung operation, very nearly killed him—within a month or two of the year for which fifteen years earlier he had jokingly predicted his death, namely, 1945, the year of the German defeat.

Like *Die Betrachtungen eines Unpolitischen* during the First World War, the Faustus novel was Mann's anguished soul-searching during the Second. While *The Magic Mountain* is a *Bildungsroman* in the tradition of *Wilhelm Meister*, much of *Doctor Faustus* seems not so much educational as didactic. The aggrieved and indignant novelist assumed the role of a *praeceptor Germaniae*, set himself up as a judge not only over Hitler's damnable Germany in particular, but over historical Germany in general. The consummate fictional form does not hide the author's strenuous intent to seek the cause of the contemporary "devil's own mess" (an expression the author often used) in the raving demons of history. In the chapters which permute themes from the Faust legend, the devil himself appears, among other impersonations as Schleppfuss [clubfoot] in a Mephistophelean mask. The poisonous infection that destroys Adrian Leverkühn by an agonizing, slow process of dissolution, is symbolically ascribed to the devil. Leverkühn, the composer possessed by the demon, has many characteristics of the philosopher Nietzsche, whose biographical data, especially those relating to his embarrassing experiences as a young man, have been taken over in part without any attempt at concealment, though the name of Nietzsche is never mentioned.

Adrian's poisoning, however, is doubly symbolic. It refers to more than the "devil's pact" that the German nation concluded with Hitler. Mann also regards as poisonous the irrational power of music which counteracts reason, "the lovely lie of sound," to use an expression of Nietzsche's. The chronicler who writes down the composer's life story is a childhood friend. Mann called him Serenus Zeitblom and drew him as a rather pedestrian sort of humanist. The choice of names in *Doctor Faustus*, incidentally, often seems somewhat artificial. In nearly all his other novels Mann had an inimitable touch in inventing characteristic names for his cast. Beginning with little Herr Friedemann, in one of the early novellas, through Tonio Kröger and Herr Spinell to Mijnheer Peeperkorn, Clavdia Chauchat, Frau Stöhr, the waiter Mager, Felix Krull and his mentor Schimmelpreester—it is a lifelong series of expert hits. But the involved and all too obviously symbolic names in *Doctor Faustus* never acquire the same unforgettable and unmistakable life.

The high-school teacher Serenus Zeitblom stands for the type of decent, educated German; as Mann sees him, he is a representative of the other Germany, perhaps even one of the "internal exiles" such as he imagined them in his exile, a minority troubled but powerless to change the course of events.

In contrast to the humanly warm, even though sometimes a little foolish and officious Serenus, Adrian comes from the "cold hell" of a man who has not got the right kind of love and through a tragic incapacity indeed cannot love at all (even in the physical sense of the word). Leverkühn, whose last work is the symphonic cantata *The Lamentation of Faust*, sums up his life in a desolate statement: "I have found that it was not to be. . . ." Zeitblom loses heart; he does not believe any more in his vocation as an educator; he has grown weary and asks himself whether there will ever be a chance again to implant in the hearts of young people "cultural ideas in which reverence for the gods of the

depths merges with the moral cult of Olympian reason
and clarity in one single faith."

The book operates on many levels and certainly
contains a number of exquisite and delightful episodes
as well as unforgettable characters. But its dark, heavy
load of ideas does not always serve it well. The satirical
picture of Munich society after the turn of the century
is not free from personal, spiteful reminiscence. And it
was not without reason that the author located the
germs of the German sickness among those circles,
which even then were given to an obscure mysticism.
Mann's just anger, his brooding melancholy, and his no
longer gentle, but often ferocious irony do not blend
well in *Doctor Faustus*. Nor is it quite clear whether
the musical theory of the twelve-tone system, to which
Mann brought a passionate meticulousness, is supposed
to have a causal or, for that matter, even a phenomeno-
logical, connection with the German catastrophe.

Mann himself provided the key to the complica-
tions and richly symbolic oddities of his *Doctor Faustus*
novel. He did so in the little book *The Story of a Novel:
The Genesis of Doctor Faustus*, which was written during the years 1943 to 1947, and published in 1949. In it
Mann acknowledges the difficulties and shortcomings
of his work. The mere fact that he followed up the
novel immediately with such an exhaustive commentary on its production, proves that the circumstances in
which he unburdened himself of the work were anything but happy. Without consideration for his admitted vanity, Mann lays his cards on the table. He
writes down a pedantic record of all the general and
private occurrences during the time he toiled on the
great novel. He never loses his calm, which indeed is
hardly disturbed even when he gets ironically cross

with himself. Let people think what they like about him! He complains about the deluge of reviews: "Such mass consumption of public utterances about a work that is completed is confusing, irritating, and extremely sterile."

The diary forestalls all critical objections. He bluntly justifies his use in the composition of the intellectual property of others, with particular reference to his studies in the theory of music: "In the artist's eyes an idea as such will never have much value either in itself or as a piece of intellectual property. What matters to him is its functional value in the intellectual mechanism of the work." Once he even says: "The technical study of music frightens and bores me." Then he records his reading in the course of his work: Kierkegaard, Shakespeare, again and again Nietzsche and, incidentally, a biography of James Joyce. In this connection he notes: "In matters of style there is really nothing but parody for me nowadays, rather like Joyce in this respect. . . ." In comparison with the Irishman's eccentric avant-gardism, he accuses himself of "feeble traditionalism." However, this had the advantage of "easier accessibility despite the tinge of parody," and of "the chance of some popularity."

He commands admiration by the way he shows us the *Poeta laureatus* without make-up, often tired, sometimes cynical, and above all stripped of his laurels. Often there is a chill in the air about him, as in the case of his Leverkühn, and he is lonely in the midst of a carefully fostered and tended social life. The immanent sorrow has a saving grace and it is touching to read how conscientiously he discharged the obligations of everyday life and convention; receptions and a crushing load of correspondence, missions, radio talks and, not last, the family duties of an exiled patriarch. His earnest descriptions of the obsequies of friends and famous fellow writers betray his satisfaction at his own durability. The remark about the death of artists, in connection with the sudden passing of Bruno Frank and Franz Werfel, is of sublime cynicism. The various distasteful ceremonies are described with relish. In his old age Thomas Mann became the realistic portraitist of exile society. Future historians will turn to him as a rich source.

The novel *Der Erwählte* (*The Holy Sinner*), published in 1951, is a characteristic sideline in Mann's output. Up to a point its subject belongs in the thematic range of the *Doctor Faustus* novel and, like it, is based on a medieval German legend—in this case on motifs from Hartmann von der Aue and from stories in the *Gesta Romanorum*. As in the *Wälsungenblut*, the novella that he wrote as a young man and then withdrew, the novel treats in mythological and psychological terms the problem of love between brother and sister. Under the cover of history, he touches upon erotic taboos, incest, and the Oedipus situation. But the tale of sin and expiation as applied to Grigorss, subsequently, as Gregorius, elevated to the Papal throne, is at heart the result not so much of the author's roaming imagination, as of his passion for experimenting with language and for exploring the mythical substrata and origins in the human soul. No doubt his linguistic studies were stimulated by exile. In *The Holy Sinner* Thomas Mann's linguistic parody reaches peaks to which the reader can climb only with the help of dictionaries and encyclopedias. The colorful mosaic of language is made up of stylized elements of courtly

Old German and Old French, church Latin and Old English clerical language (the narrator is an Irish monk), spiced with anachronistic wit in which Low German is mixed with American slang.

Even more patently than *Doctor Faustus*, the later novel displays the author's tendency to undermine myth and mysticism by depth psychology and satire. What he said in 1936 in his speech on *Freud und die Zukunft* (*Freud and the Future*) about the psychological motives for illuminating the mythical, gives a particularly clear picture of his attitude to scientific research, in which he saw an instrument of reason and enlightenment. The following sentences from this famous speech on Freud constitute, as it were, an introduction to the far-ranging intellectual expeditions of Mann's "mythical novels," from the Joseph tetralogy to *The Holy Sinner*.

Analytical insights change the world; they beget a serene suspicion, a distrust which unmasks the hideouts and machinations of the psyche. Once awakened, it can never again disappear from the world. It infiltrates life, undermines its crude naïveness, removes from it the intenseness of ignorance, makes it dispassionate by cultivating a taste for "understatement," as the English say, for forms of expression that understate rather than overstate, for the use of temperate, uninflated words which take their strength from moderation. . . . It should never be forgotten that the German word *Bescheidenheit* (modesty) comes from *Bescheidwissen* (cognizance of), that this was its original meaning from which subsequently it derived its secondary meaning of modesty, moderation. Modesty from knowledge—let us assume that this will be the underlying mood of a serenely sobered world of peace, which the science of the unconscious may well be called upon to help bring about.

It may have been an act of self-liberation for
Thomas Mann to get back to a "light" subject after the
late and tragic adventures of his life, of exile, and after
his stupendous intellectual expeditions into history and
prehistory, cultural philosophy and depth psychology.
Confessions of Felix Krull, Confidence Man is humor
in the finest sense of the word.

As often happened with Thomas Mann, this novel,
of which we have to be satisfied with only the first part,
was the outcome of projects which occupied the author
for years, not to say all his life. In the case of *Felix
Krull* a fragment was written as early as before the
First World War; although interrupted for years and
then at last resumed, the work has nothing stale about
it, thanks to the zest, the joyous zest for life, whose
source is humor. Its true mark is not loud laughter, but
the quietly happy smile. Instead of sketching his characters after some model, as in nearly all other cases,
the author here deals with a freely invented figure, and
take such pleasure in him that it at once infects the
reader, whose possible moral misgivings (is not a thief
and impostor raised to the status of a "hero"?) are
allayed by sheer delight in beauty, by love of life
beyond good and evil.

But then, Felix Krull is no common criminal, just
as the tale of his strange life has not the remotest re-
semblance to an ordinary crime novel. Felix means
happy, lucky; and the lucky Felix Krull possesses in a
high degree what Goethe once, somewhat mysteriously, called "inborn merit." At first sight Felix gets
everything seemingly without effort, despite the handi-
cap of a childhood oppressed by poverty and family
distress. He gains the favor of women, the protection
of rich and powerful men. His dreams come true of

themselves, he makes the brilliant pseudocareer of a prince of confidence men, upon whom the role of man of the world is inescapably forced. But at the bottom of his heart this charming and urbane mischief-maker is an admirer and dependable adherent of the doomed social order around the turn of the century. Loosely connected, one exquisite episode follows another to form a chain of small adventures born of impish high spirits. Among the high points are Krull, no less cunning than Schweik, bamboozling the draft board; Krull, a hotel page in Paris, doted on by infatuated society ladies; Krull, the waiter, exchanging his tail coat with that of a nobleman and getting a decoration from a king for the jokes with which he cheers up the careworn monarch. . . .

It goes without saying, incidentally, that Mann did not fail to introduce educational conversations into his picaresque novel. He did so in the most charming manner. The language he used for the purpose is parodistical and entertaining, like the prose of his later years in general. He delighted in making fun of the language of the century in which, after all, he had grown up, by parodying the stilted and mannered expression, the conventional phrase. It almost seems as though Mann were amused at his own lecturing; that would be the stroke of genius of sovereign humor, and would deflate his opponents. With Felix Krull Mann dons the clothes of one of Fortune's spoiled darlings. They suit him very well.

10

Epílogue

Mann never settled again in Germany after the collapse of the Hitler regime, but visited his country only on a few lecture tours. When he was deprived of his citizenship in 1936, President Beneš conferred Czechoslovak nationality on him and his family.

In June 1944 he became a citizen of the United States. An entry in his diary records how deeply moved he was by the ceremony of taking the oath in Los Angeles, and adds that he was pleased at the idea that he should have become an American in Roosevelt's time.

It would be rather pointless in a literary and psychological study of an author the intellectual significance and artistic status of whose work have long ceased to be debatable, to discuss in addition the changing political aspects of his writings and public pronouncements.

Yet it was doubtless those aspects that impaired Mann's popularity in Germany after the Second World War, and that caused his friend the writer Hermann Hesse to say in his obituary of Mann that the author of the *Doctor Faustus* novel and of the transatlantic radio talks *An meine deutschen Hörer* [To My German Listeners], had been "misunderstood" in his alleged lack of patriotism.

Over and over again doubts have been cast upon Mann's right to assume the role of a political prophet insofar as his judgments (and condemnations) were colored by the grievances of an exile, of a "neo-American" of the Roosevelt era. But more than once in crucial phases of political change he had felt obliged to speak up as a prophet, a mentor and warner. He met the claims of the day with the voice of a free con-

science. However much certain remarks in his numerous speeches, letters, articles, and interviews may have
been colored by the passion of current controversies,
some of his great historical and political essays point
the way beyond the present to a better future for his
own nation and the whole of mankind.

In the address *Deutschland und die Deutschen*
(*Germany and the Germans*), which he delivered on
his seventieth birthday, in 1945, at the Library of
Congress in Washington, he found words inspired
not by hatred but love of Germany, words that advised
the Germans to go beyond "bourgeois democracy" and
strive for "social humanism," rejecting all violent totalitarian solutions. And he concluded:

In its [Germany's] aversion to the world there was always
so much longing for the world, at the bottom of the loneli-
ness which made it wicked, so much—which of us can fail
to know it?—of a desire to love, a desire to be loved.
Ultimately the German misfortune is only the paradigm
of the tragedy of the human condition as such.

Mann's view of the world was one that fused
humanity and politics in the light of modern knowledge
and scientific experience. In order not merely to "understand" that view, but to grasp it—insofar as it is not
sufficiently clear from his fiction—we should perhaps
turn to *Meine Zeit* (*The Years of My Life*), a lecture
delivered at Chicago in 1950, which contains the dis-
tilled wisdom of his old age.

In it, Mann frankly confessed his allegiance to the
nineteenth century's cultural values, to its "sense of
greatness," and its bourgeois liberalism. "The years of
my life—they were eventful, but my life is a unity."

These were the words of an author who deliberately wrote no autobiography, "after so many books made out of my life."

We cannot interpret and explain Thomas Mann's *œuvre* better or more tellingly than he does himself. His life, his work and thought, including his political thought with its occasionally distorted but essentially clear appreciation of world affairs, must be taken as a whole. In his meditations on the classical postulates of the old bourgeois society, Thomas Mann strove for a synthesis of the liberal, though often mutually exclusive, theses of freedom and equality.

In the reminiscences, *The Years of My Life,* Mann declared himself against any exaggerated concept of freedom, which tended toward anarchy, as he was also against any sort of totalitarian, dogmatic leveling. Totalitarianism especially, in every shape or form, came in for his sharpest condemnation, because of its "fundamental incompatibility with truth." "As a novelist, psychologist, and portrayer of things human," he protested, "I am pledged to truth and dependent upon it."

This is a repudiation of any form of dictatorship, which, for the rulers and subjects alike, necessarily implies the obligation of mendacity.

Two solemn occasions took Thomas Mann back to his native country, in each case for a short while. In 1949 he went to Frankfurt to receive the Goethe prize, as a gesture of reconciliation on both sides. In May 1955 he made his last appearance as the state's official speaker at a celebration, as he had done so often before with outstanding distinction. The address was delivered at Stuttgart and bore the title *Versuch über Schiller, Seinem Andenken in Liebe gewidmet* [An

Essay on Schiller, Dedicated to His Memory with Affection]. The concluding sentences of this unforgettable appeal have all the marks of Thomas Mann's own spiritual legacy to the nation, pronounced under the shadow of imminent death:

As we commemorate his burial and resurrection, may something of his gentle and powerful will enter into us, something of his will to beauty, truth and goodness, to morality and inner freedom, to art, to love, to peace, and to the saving grace of human self-respect.

Thomas Mann, who in this wonderful message of timeless humanity once more addressed a call for unity to the German people in the name of its poet, died at Zurich on August 12, 1955, mourned by Germans in both parts of their divided country.

Chronology

1875:   Born at Lübeck on June 6

1890:   Death of his father, Senator Heinrich Mann

1893:   Move to Munich and job as an apprentice clerk in a fire insurance company

1894:   The story "Gefallen" published in the review *Gesellschaft* (edited by M. G. Conrad). Encouraging letter from Richard Dehmel

1898:   Volume of short stories *Der kleine Herr Friedemann, und andere Novellen*

1900:   Military service

1901:   *Buddenbrooks. Verfall einer Familie*

1903:   *Tristan: Sechs Novellen*

1905:   Marriage with Katharina Pringsheim

1905:   *Fiorenza*, drama

1906:   *Wälsungenblut* (withdrawn)

1909:   *Königliche Hoheit,* novel

1912:   *Der Tod in Venedig*

1915:   "Friedrich und die große Koalition"

1918:   *Betrachtungen eines Unpolitischen*

1919:   *Herr und Hund, Gesang vom Kindchen,* two idylls

1922:   "Von deutscher Republik," speech

1923:   "Goethe und Tolstoi," lecture delivered in 1921

103

1924:   *Der Zauberberg,* novel
1925:   *Unordnung und frühes Leid*
1926:   *Pariser Rechenschaft*
1929:   Award of the Nobel Prize for Literature
1930:   *Mario und der Zauberer*
1930:   *Lebensabriß*
1932:   "Goethe als Repräsentant des bürgerlichen
        Zeitalters"
1933–1943:   *Joseph und seine Brüder*
            I. *Die Geschichten Jaakobs,* Berlin, 1933
            II. *Der junge Joseph,* Berlin, 1934
            III. *Joseph in Ägypten,* Vienna, 1936
            IV. *Joseph der Ernährer,* Stockholm, 1943
1935:   *Leiden und Größe der Meister,* essays
1936:   Loss of German citizenship
1938:   Move to United States (Pacific Palisades near Los
        Angeles, California)
1939:   *Lotte in Weimar,* published in Stockholm
1939:   *Das Problem der Freiheit,* in the series *Ausblicke,*
        Stockholm
1941:   *Die vertauschten Köpfe: Eine indische Legende*
1943:   *Das Gesetz: Erzählung*
1947:   *Doktor Faustus,* novel
1949:   *Die Entstehung des Doktor Faustus: Roman eines
        Romans*
1949:   First visit to Germany after the war. Address
        during the Goethe-year celebrations (Frankfurt,
        July 23, 1949)
1950:   *Meine Zeit,* address at the University of Chicago
1952:   Move to Kilchberg near Zürich
1953:   *Die Betrogene: Erzählung*
1954:   *Bekenntnisse des Hochstaplers Felix Krull. Der
        Memoiren erster Teil.* (Revised version that in-
        cluded editions published in 1922, 1936, 1954.)
1955:   *Versuch über Schiller: Seinem Andenken zum 150.
        Todestag*
1955:   Died August 12 in Zurich

Bibliography

Works by Thomas Mann

Der kleine Herr Friedemann, novellas, 1898 (Little Herr Friedemann, in *Stories of Three Decades*, 1936)

Buddenbrooks, novel, 1901 (*Buddenbrooks*, 1924)

Tristan, novellas, 1903. Includes inter alia: *Tonio Kröger* and *Tristan* (both translated in *Stories of Three Decades*, 1936)

Fiorenza, drama, 1905

Königliche Hoheit, novella, 1909 (*Royal Highness*, 1916)

Der Tod in Venedig, novella, 1911 (*Death in Venice*, 1925; also in *Stories of Three Decades*, 1936)

Das Wunderkind, novellas, 1914

Die Betrachtungen eines Unpolitischen, autobiographical reflections, 1918

Herr und Hund, idyl, 1918 (*Bashan and I*, 1923; also in *Stories of Three Decades*, 1936)

Gesang vom Kindchen, idyll, 1919

Wälsungenblut, story, 1921

Gesammelte Werke, 15 vols., 1922–35

Rede und Antwort, essays, 1922. Includes: *Bilse und ich*; *Versuch über das Theater*; *Der alte Fontane* (The Old Fontane, in *Stories of Three Decades*, 1936); *Friedrich und die große Koalition* (Frederick and the Great Coalition, in *Three Essays*, 1929)

Erzählungen, 2 vols., 1922. Includes: *Enttäuschung; Der Bajazzo; Der Weg zum Friedhof; Gladius Dei; Ein Glück; Beim Propheten; Schwere Stunde; Das Eisenbahnunglück*

Die Bekenntnisse des Hochstaplers Felix Krull, novel, 1922; enlarged, 1936; new version, 1954 (*Confessions of Felix Krull, Confidence Man,* 1955)

Der Zauberberg, novel, 1924 (*The Magic Mountain,* 1927)

Vom Geist der Medizin, essay, 1925

Bemühungen, essays, 1925. Includes inter alia: *Goethe und Tolstoi; Okkulte Erlebnisse* (Goethe and Tolstoy, and An Experience in the Occult, in *Three Essays,* 1929); *Von deutscher Republik*

Pariser Rechenschaft, travelogue, 1926

Unordnung und frühes Leid, novella, 1926 (*Early Sorrow,* 1929; also in *Stories of Three Decades,* 1936)

Deutsche Ansprache: Ein Appell an die Vernunft, lecture, 1930

Lebensabriß, autobiographical sketch, 1930 (*A Sketch of My Life,* 1960)

Mario und der Zauberer, novella, 1930 (*Mario and the Magician,* 1930)

Die Forderung des Tages, political essays, 1930 (*Order of the Day: Political Essays and Speeches of Two Decades,* 1942). Includes: *Kultur und Sozialismus; Die Stellung Freuds in der modernen Geistesgeschichte; Lübeck als geistige Lebensform; Rede über Lessing*

Joseph und seine Brüder, novel, 4 vols., 1933–43 (*Joseph and His Brothers,* 1934–45): Vol. I, *Die Geschichten Jaakobs* (*The Tales of Jacob*); Vol. II, *Der junge Joseph* (*The Young Joseph*); Vol. III, *Joseph in Ägypten* (*Joseph in Egypt*); Vol. IV, *Joseph der Ernährer* (*Joseph the Provider*)

Leiden und Größe der Meister, essays, 1395. Includes: *Goethe als Repräsentant des bürgerlichen Zeitalters; Goethes Laufbahn als Schriftsteller; Leiden und Größe Richard Wagners; Meerfahrt mit Don Quijote*

(Goethe as Representative of the Bourgeois Age; Goethe's Career as Man of Letters; The Suffering and Greatness of Richard Wagner, Voyage with Don Quixote, in *Essays of Three Decades*, 1947); *August von Platen*; *Theodor Storm*

Freud und die Zukunft, lecture, 1936 (Freud and the Future, in *Essays of Three Decades*, 1947)

Ein Briefwechsel, letters, 1937 (*An Exchange of Letters*, 1937). Correspondence with the Dean of the Philosophy Department, University of Bonn, when Mann's name was taken off the roster of honorary doctors

Dieser Friede, essay, 1938 (*This Peace*, 1938)

Achtung, Europa!, manifesto, 1938

Vom zukünftigen Sieg der Demokratie, lecture, 1938 (*The Coming Victory of Democracy*, 1938)

Schopenhauer, essays, 1938

Das Problem der Freiheit, essay, 1939

Die Kunst des Romans, essay, 1939

Lotte in Weimar, novel, 1939 (*The Beloved Returns: Lotte in Weimar*, 1940)

Die vertauschten Köpfe; *Eine indische Legende*, story, 1940 (*The Transposed Heads: A Legend of India*, 1941)

Dieser Krieg, lecture, 1940 (*This War*, 1940)

Deutsche Hörer, radio talks, 1944; enlarged, 1945

Das Gesetz, story, 1944 (*The Tables of the Law*, 1945)

Ausgewählte Erzählungen, 1945

Adel des Geistes. Sechzehn Versuche zum Problem der Humanität, essays, 1945

Deutschland und die Deutschen, speech, 1947

Meistererzählungen, 1947

Doktor Faustus, novel, 1947 (*Doctor Faustus*, 1949)

Neue Studien, essays, 1948. Includes: *Phantasie über Goethe*; *Dostojewskij-mit Maßen*; *Nietzsches Philosophie im Lichte unserer Erfahrung*

Goethe und die Demokratie, speech, 1949

Ansprache im Goethejahr 1949, speech, 1949

Die Entstehung des Doktor Faustus: Roman eines Romans,
    1949 (*The Story of a Novel: The Genesis of Doctor
    Faustus*, 1961)
Meine Zeit, lecture, 1950 (The Years of My Life, in
    Harper's Magazine, 1950)
Michelangelo in seinen Dichtungen, essays, 1950
Der Erwählte, novella, 1951 (*The Holy Sinner*, 1952),
    based on Hartmann von Aue
Lob der Vergänglichkeit, essay, 1952
Der Künstler und die Gesellschaft, speech, 1952
Gerhart Hauptmann, speech, 1953
Altes und Neues, short prose pieces, 1953
Die Betrogene, story, 1953 (*The Black Swan*, 1954)
Ansprache im Schillerjahr 1955, speech, 1955
Versuch über Schiller, essays, 1955; play, 1956 (*On
    Schiller*, 1958)
Nachlese Prosa 1951–1955, 1957
Erzählungen, stories, 1958
Briefe an Paul Amann, 1951–1952, ed. H. Wegener, 1959
Gesammelte Werke in 12 Bänden, 1960
Thomas Mann and Ernst Bertram, 1910–1955, 1960
*Thomas Mann-Karl Kereyi: Gespräch in Briefen 1934–
    1955*, 1960
Briefe, letters, ed. Erika Mann, 3 vols., 1961–65
Thomas Mann-Robert Faesi: Briefwechsel, letters, 1962
Thomas Mann-Heinrich Mann: Briefwechsel 1900–1945,
    letters, ed. Klaus Mann, 1965
Das essayistische Werk, ed. Hans Bürgin, 8 vols., 1968

Works about Thomas Mann

Alegria, Fernando. *Ensayo sobre cinco temas de Thomas
    Mann.* 1949
Brennan, Joseph. *Thomas Mann's World.* 1942
Bürgin, Hans, and Hans-Otto Mayer. *Thomas Mann: A
    Chronicle of His Life.* 1969

Cassirer, Ernst. "Thomas Manns Goethebild, eine Studie über *Lotte in Weimar*." *Germanic Review* 20 (1945)

Eloesser, A. *Thomas Mann: Sein Leben und sein Werk*. 1925

Faesi, Robert. *Thomas Mann*. 1955

Fougere, J. *Thomas Mann, ou La Seduction de la mort*. 1947

Hamburger, Käte. *Thomas Mann und die Romantik*. 1932
——. *Manns Roman "Joseph und seine Brüder."* 1945

Hatfield, Henry. *Thomas Mann*. 1951
——, ed. *Thomas Mann*. 1964

Heller, Erich. *Disinherited Mind*. 1957
——. *The Ironic German: A Study of Thomas Mann*. 1958

Hellersberg-Wendriner, A. *Mystik der Gottesferne*. 1960

Jonas, Klaus W. *Fifty Years of Thomas Mann Studies: A Bibliography*. 1955

Kahler, Erich. *Orbit of Thomas Mann*. 1969

Kantorowicz, A. *Heinrich und Thomas Mann*. 1956

Lesser, J. *Thomas Mann in der Epoche seiner Vollendung*. 1952

Lukacs, Georg. *Essays on Thomas Mann*. 1957

Mann, Erika. *Das letzte Jahr*. 1956

Mann, Heinrich, *Mein Bruder*. 1955

Mann, V. *Wir waren Fünf: Bildnis der Familie Mann*. 1949

Mayer, Hans. *Thomas Mann: Sein Leben und Werk*. 1950
——. *Leiden und Größe Thomas Manns*. 1956

Neider, Charles, ed. *The Stature of Thomas Mann*. 1947

Perl, W. H. *Thomas Mann 1933–1945: Vom deutschen Humanisten zum amerikanischen Weltbürger*. 1945

Strich, Fritz. *Kunst und Leben*. 1960

Thomas, R. Hinton. *Thomas Mann: The Mediation of Art*. 1956

Weigand, Hermann. *Magic Mountain: A Study of Thomas Mann's Novel "Der Zauberberg."* 1964

Wolff, H. M. *Thomas Mann: Werk und Bekenntnis*. 1957

Index